Stock Market Baseball

How trading for singles, doubles, triples,

and an occasional home run,

can win the stock market game

By John George Campbell

Published by John George Campbell 2013

Copyright © 2013 John George Campbell
All rights reserved.

First Paperback Edition December 2013

TD Ameritrade, Inc. and John George Campbell are separate unaffiliated companies and are not responsible for each others' services or policies.
© 2013 TD Ameritrade IP Company, Inc. Used with permission.
For illustrative purposes only.

ISBN:1494405865
ISBN-13:978-1494405861

DEDICATION

This book is dedicated
to my family.

Discuss your game plan at
http://stockmarketbaseball.com/

CONTENTS

"You're always trying to hit a home run." 11

Looking for your pitch 15

Things I look for when choosing a stock that I want to trade. 17

    OBV. On Balance Volume. 17

    How many shares are in the float? 19

    Crossing patterns. 21

    The Share price. 23

    RSI. The Relative Strength Index. 24

    Fibonacci retrace-ment Levels. 25

    MACD and Stochastics 25

    Bollinger Bands. 26

Stock Market Baseball Scorecard. 30

One percent a day 33

Potential Daily, Weekly, and Annual returns making 1%, 2%, or 3% a day 37

    Daily return on investment, based on amount invested, and % returned on that investment, per week. 38

    Weekly return on investment, based on amount invested, and % returned on that investment, per week. 39

    Annual return on investment, based on the amount invested, and the percentage returned on that investment, per day. 40

When to hit the long ball, and go for extra bases. 44

The BIG Grand Slam 48

    The Golden Cross 48

- Cup and Handle 50
- Inverted Head and Shoulders..52
- Reverse Gap up...54

HGSI Grand Slam Play by Play...56

But the markets STINK !!!! So, go short ! 65

But I'm not rich ! I can't afford to play the game ! 68

Focus on technical indicators..73

Scouting the Prospects..75

Get in the game, Rookie..80
- Use limit trades...84
- Don't use market orders. 85
- Use GTC, Good Till Canceled orders..................................86
- Sell Short, if you can't go long...86
- Always double check your order entry for price, and amount of shares to be traded. 87

You can't win them all 88
- Use Stop Losses. 90
- Use mental stops 90

" But, that's not fair !"..93
- Choose your entry and exit targets carefully. 94
- Diversify. 95
- Use Calls and Puts...96
- "Cut your losses and let your winners run". 97

Keep your head in the game...101

But the game is fixed. I can't compete................................105

Game Day 109

4:30 AM, PST . (Pacific Standard Time) 110

5:00 AM, PST to 6:30AM, PST. 110

6:30 AM, PST. 111

7:30AM, PST. 114

9:00AM to 10:00AM, PST 115

10:00 AM, PST to 1PM, PST. 115

1:00 PM to 2:00 PM, PST. 116

2:00 PM to 5:00PM, PST. 117

Succeed because you "Have to" 119

Use Technical analysis to help you score at Stock Market Baseball 124

Dream. Dream Big 125

About the Author 128

Endnotes and LINKS 129

"You're always trying to hit a home run."

Those are the words that one of my friends said to me when we were discussing my investment style. And he was right. I'm always looking to hit a home run, or a four bagger, when I'm assessing an investment in a stock. Who wouldn't want a 400% return on their investment? But how often does that happen in the financial markets? Enough times to make it worth my while to look. I've had several investments increase by 200% to 300% in a relatively short period of time. Say, over the span of a few weeks, or months. In 2009 I started to trade HGSI, Human Genome Science, right after it had gapped up from 88 cents to $1.31. I traded it off, and on, through the low 2 dollar range, and bought my final shares in the mid 2 dollar range. That was in May of 2009. I sold my last shares in HGSI between $26.50 and $28.50. My overall gain, on a good portion of my shares, was over 1200 %, within a nine month period of time. So finding those pots of gold is doable, as long as you understand that it may take several months to payoff. Or years.

If you like to trade, and buying and holding is just plain boring for you, you might want to take my friend's baseball reference a few steps further, and start to think of the trading game like the game of baseball. What's the object of the game of baseball? To score runs, and win the game, right? How do the good teams do that? By moving their runners along the base path until they've crossed home plate. Do they do that by hitting home runs all the time? No. What do some of the well managed, winning teams, do to win the game of baseball? They play small ball. They hit a lot of singles, quite a few doubles, fewer triples, and every now and then, a home run. There are a lot of ways to win at the game of baseball, and there are a lot of ways to win at he game of Stock Market Baseball too! The key is to score runs.

What constitutes a run? Four singles will produce a run, and keep you in scoring position to keep on putting runners across home plate. Two doubles will do that too. A triple and a single could push a runner across home plate too. And a home run is sweet whenever you can make them happen. But most of the time, you win at the game of baseball by hitting a lot of singles and doubles.

So, how does that equate to winning at the game of stock trading, or commodity trading, or any sort of investment platform that can be traded daily? Well, as any trader can tell you, a good day in the market can be had on as little as a 1% gain on your investment, depending on the amount invested. And there are a lot of stocks that move higher, or lower, than 1% in a given day. There are others that move 2% to 5%, and more, though they are a bit harder to come by. But they do come by. I've owned stocks that moved up over 400% in one day. Many move up 20% to 50% on positive news that effects their companies. But let's not get ahead of ourselves. Let's focus on getting on base.

A 1% gain equals a single.

That would make a 2% gain in a day a double.

A 3% gain in a day, would be a triple.

A 4% gain would put you on the scoreboard.

Why? Because, for the sake of the game of Stock Market Baseball, you just scored a run, and runs help you win the game. In all actuality the percentage you make a day, week, month, and year is what you really need to keep your focus on.

Think about this. If you make 1% a day on your trade, and you do that 5 times in a week, you just scored a run in Stock Market Baseball, and a 5% return on your investment in a week. Now, extrapolate that 5% gain over 52 weeks and you've made 260% over the course of a year, and that's just based on 1% each trading day, multiplied by 5 days a week. Though you may not be able to hit a single every day, it's really not that big of a goal to achieve. It's doable.

Look. I'm no professionally trained stock trader, or sophisticated hedge fund manager. No one showed me the basics of how to read a chart, or explained to me anything about technical analysis. Most of this information I taught myself, and there's a lot that I still don't know. But in 2008, while still trading on a part time basis, the majority of my completed trades ended with me making money. In 2009, when I finally started trading on a full time basis, out of sheer necessity, because my financial and personal life had my back against a wall, my portfolio ended up 550 % higher than where it started at the beginning of the year, even after cashing out over $114,000.00 worth of gains.

There are many other men and women, with more professional experience in the markets, but very, very few of them, beat my performance in 2009. Very few of them, if any, beat a 550% gain in their portfolio value, after taking out $114,00.00 to live on and help pay down past debts. 2010 is looked good too. I'm thankful to the numerous investment blogs, and investment sites, that have helped a regular guy like me succeed in trading the market, and giving me the tools to do so. Without their online training, and sites explaining technical analysis of investments, I would never have dug out of the deep financial hole that I was in. And most of this information and education is free, if you know how to search for it on the internet.

I hope that my story, and methods, learned by actual experience, can help other people, just like me, to understand that trading stocks in the stock markets is not something just reserved for the wealthy, Wall Street types, or the well connected. I'm living proof that a regular guy, or gal, can do it too, and profit greatly. Even in these challenging financial times.

Look for your pitch

©2013 John George Campbell   stockmarketbaseball.com

Looking for your pitch

It's been quite a few years since I played a game of baseball, but when I did, I remember that I was coached to wait for my pitch. Just don't swing at anything thrown your way. Wait for a pitch that you think you can hit, with the objective of getting on base and moving the other runners on base further along into scoring position, or across home plate.

In Stock Market Baseball, the advice is the same. Don't swing at all the stocks you think are going to be the home run ball. You might get fooled, and strike out. Wait on your pitch. So what does that mean? For the sake of staying in the game every day, I look for stocks that look to be making a move, up, or down. Because in

Stock Market Baseball, you don't always have to be long on a stock and make money when the share price rises. You can score, and make money, when you go short, and the share price falls in value, too. It's not just about the direction of the trade that helps you score in Stock Market Baseball. It's the percentage of the move, and how you played it, long, or short, that helps you to score and make money in Stock Market Baseball.

    How do you find the right pitch? Since the game of Stock Market Baseball is meant to be played on a daily, or weekly, basis, I use a few tools to help me scout the right stocks, or pitches, to hit. First of all, I use Technical Analysis to help me find the stocks I want to play with. I don't want to play all the stocks in the market, and I don't want to spend too much time over-analyzing all of their fundamental values, since I might only be playing them for a day, or week, or so. Technical indicators work well for me when I'm considering what stocks to play. Think of this process like scouting baseball prospects. Take a little time to see what the stock has going for it, but most of all, look for what kind of momentum that stock's share price is showing to you now, up, or down, based on recent activity.

Things I look for when choosing a stock that I want to trade.

OBV. On Balance Volume.

Has the average daily volume for the stock increased by 100%, 200%, or more, over the last few days, weeks and months? I want to know this, since it's a sign to me that investors and money are either flowing to, or out of, the stock. That kind of volume action can help you to estimate which way the stock will continue to move in.

One other aspect about volume that I look for is how many shares that trade daily. I don't want to be trapped in a stock trading less than 250,000 shares daily, at the very least. And especially none that trade less than 100,000 shares daily. Why? Because, if I'm wrong, and the trade starts to work against me there may not be enough buyers to take my shares off my hands, and I could get trapped holding those shares for a long time. Another thing to consider, if you have more money to invest and play the Stock Market Baseball game with, is that with the more shares you own of a thinly traded, low float company, the more you can be putting yourself at risk of being trapped with those shares if no one else comes along to take them off your hands.

For example, a guy with only $25,000 to trade with, fully

invested in a $2.00 stock, with an average daily volume of 250,000 shares traded, would control 12,500 shares of the average daily volume of that $2.00 stock. Or, about 5% of the overall daily volume traded in that $2.00 stock. The likelihood that the guy with $25,000 to trade. and ownership of 5% of this $2.00 stock getting in, and then getting out, in the same day, is risky, but reasonably good. Just keep in my mind that his initial buy of 12,500 shares, and subsequent sale of 12,500 shares will represent 10% of the average daily volume traded at the end of the day, since he will have accounted for 25,000 shares of that daily volume traded. Now consider a guy with $100,000.00 to trade with. If he buys into the $2.00 stock and takes control of 50,000 shares, his buy will equate to 20% of the entire average daily volume. The odds that he'll be able to find a buyer, in the same day, to take those same 50,000 shares off of his hands, are much less than the guy trading with only $25,000, because the larger investor has more exposure to the entire average daily volume, and may not find buyers for all of his shares in the same day that he bought them. Taking this one step further, if this trader was able to find a buyer, or buyers, his initial buy and subsequent sale of shares in that $2.00 stock that day would equate to 40% of the average daily volume. That's a very foolish play, in my opinion, since the odds of him getting in, and out, with that percentage of the day's shares in his control, are pretty low. So, for the guy with $100,000.00 to trade with, it would probably be better to find a stock with at least a $5.00 floor on the price, and probably 500,000 shares traded, on average, per day. The odds of getting in, and out, of a stock are more in your favor the less percentage exposure your shares represent as a portion of the overall average daily volume.

How many shares are in the float?

The float is the entire amount of shares available to freely trade in the market. When the powers of supply and demand take effect on shares of a stock with a low float, dynamic, and dramatic moves in the share price can be experienced.. The fewer shares in the float, the more dramatic a move in the share price can be, on good news.

For example, demand for shares of a company with less than 20 million shares in the float would put more upward pressure on the share price than it would have for a company with 100,000,000 shares in the float. However, there may be very good reasons why one company has fewer shares in the float than the other. Maybe it has no institutional investors. Maybe it doesn't have a strong following, or appears to be, fundamentally, a very risky investment, and investors and traders have been avoiding it. Maybe the company with the larger float has a much broader following, a much better management team, and a more high profile product or business plan that has caught the imagination of traders and investors, and 100,000,000 shares in the float doesn't seem too large of a float, since the company may trade several million shares a day, while the smaller company might only trade a couple hundred thousand shares a day, on average.. But, all things being equal, the effect of supply and demand on companies with a lower float, on the heels of good news, will be more pronounced and dramatic than for a company with a larger amount of shares in the float. Here's a real world example. Pharmathene, (PIP), on October 15th, 2010, spiked 61% on the heels of an article published on a heavily followed investment investment blog pertaining to speculation that Pharmathene was likely to win a court trial that wasn't even scheduled to start until January 2011, with another hot company, SIGA, that had already jumped in share price value over 50% earlier in that same week, on news of a huge 2.8 billion dollar contract for a smallpox anti-viral that SIGA had developed with the financial assistance from the US Government. Pharmathene had 14.5 million shares in the float when this occurred. SIGA had 30 million shares in it's float. Pip traded over 26 millions shares of it's float, on Thursday, October 14th, and on Friday, October 15th, combined. Both PIP's, and SIGA's experience, represent how big news, even a positive speculative rumor, can have a dynamic effect on the share price of a company with a low float.

Crossing patterns.

What I look for, in either a short term prospect, or longer term prospect, is a chart pattern referred to as a Golden Cross. That's the 50 day moving average crossing above the 200 day moving average. The reason this is important to me is because the 50 day moving average represents recent momentum of the share price, on an upward trajectory, through a longer term 200 day moving average, that has acted like a ceiling, or resistance, to the stock price, for more than 6 months. Breaking through, and above, this 200 day moving average barrier is kind of a big deal, and could be suggestive of better things to come for the stock, and share price. A stock showing this pattern is one I would consider going long in. Conversely, in a down market, I might want to look for a stock whose 50 day moving average is falling below the 200 day moving average, since it's just fallen below long term support, and may very well continue to fall. In that case I would consider playing that stock short. That set up of the 50 day moving average falling below the 200 day moving average is called a Death Cross. When the market is falling, as well as the share price of many stocks, as it was in 2008, I would look for stocks showing those downward moving trend lines, and choose which stocks to trade short.

Another crossing pattern that you might want to consider is the 12 day moving average crossing the 26 day moving average, since that price direction indicates recent price action and momentum. The reason I don't use it much is because the 50 day crossing the

200 day is a more significant occurrence, in my opinion, and since there are so many stocks to consider, the 50 day crossing the 200 day seems to work well for me in cutting down on the number of stocks to consider. There's just so few hours in a day, and so many stocks to analyze, so this cuts down on those I need to research. Other traders have patterns that are their favorites . The Golden Cross is one of mine.

The Share price.

You can play stock market baseball with any priced stock, from penny stocks, priced below a dollar, to richly priced stocks like Google, priced above $500 a share, but what I look for are stocks priced between $2.00 and $20.00 a share. That range provides more than enough risk/reward ratio on the lower end, and enough sense of safety on the high end, to be worth my while playing. Why do I say that the lower priced stocks have a higher risk reward ratio? Because, between $2.00 and $5.00, they aren't that far removed from being actual penny stocks, and most mutual funds have policies in place that forbid them from investing in these low priced stocks until they've risen above $5.00 in share price. Hedge funds might have different standards, but most mutual funds, and institutional fund managers have to show that they are being somewhat prudent with investor's dollars, so they won't take big positions in sub $5.00 dollar stocks, if at all. So why should you? Because dynamic percentage growth can be achieved in these $2.00 to $5.00 stocks. And that's what we're after in Stock Market Baseball. Percentage moves.

For example, a 10 cent move in a $2.00 stock would make you 5% . A 10 cent move on a $10.00 stock gains you only 1%. The safer play is the $10.00 stock, but the higher risk/reward ratio is with the $2.00 stock. If you're someone who can accept greater risk, then the lower priced stock might be one you won't mind trading. If you're more concerned about minimizing your risk, while making your trade, the higher priced stock in that $2.00 to $20.00 range is probably the better trade for you. Why? Because it's very likely, that stocks with share prices between $5.00 and $20.00 have some institutional funds investing in them, and perhaps a few analysts covering their status. The likelihood of finding a market for your shares is better, as long as you invest in companies that show a decent average daily volume figure. These precautions don't remove all risk. They just help to manage, and minimize, risk. In all cases, you can lose money in the stock market, just as easy as you can make it, so figure out what kind of risk that you can personally handle, and play Stock Market Baseball accordingly. Also remember that a 5% gain on a $2.00 dollar stock, could just as easily become a 5% loss, so approach the lower dollar stock plays accordingly.

RSI. The Relative Strength Index.

I refer to this tool in order to get a better handle on when a good time to enter a trade might be. When the RSI on a daily chart is low, below 30, I might want to consider buying. When it's above 70, I would consider selling. Why? Because when the daily RSI falls below 30 it indicates that the stock is currently oversold, and when it's above 70, overbought. Sometimes there are very good reasons for the stock to be oversold, like terrible news, or overbought, like great news, but in the absence of news, I take those RSI levels as buy and sell indicators.

Fibonacci retrace-ment Levels.

Leonardo Fibonacci (1170 -1250) came up with a mathematical model illustrating the statistical likelihood of certain things to occur, and re-occur, in nature, like the increase, or decline, of rabbits breeding. Applied to stock charts I use Fibonacci retrace-ment levels to trace from the bottom of an extended move, to the top of that move, to arrive at mathematical points of support and resistance between the bottom of a run, or rally, and the top. Why? Because, with this information, I can get a better visual handle on where a stock's share price might revert back to, and test for support, or run up to, and test, for resistance. Why is this important? Because it gives me a better idea of when I should enter a trade, or exit a trade, based on Fibonacci levels of support, or resistance. One other thing to consider when using Fibonacci levels is that many professional traders use them. Many algorithmic trading software programs use them. Why shouldn't you? They help you to not fly blind when trying to determine where levels of support and resistance, and the top and bottom, of a move might be.

MACD and Stochastics.

I'm addressing both of these technical indicators together because when you bring up these common technical tools on a stock chart you can visually see when a short term movement is happening . These movements, illustrated in a very visual and linear manner, can help you to decide when to buy or sell. MACD, or Moving Average Convergence Divergence, lines can clearly indicate when a deviation in the trend line of the stock price is occurring. The MACD shows two different lines. When the lines trend closely together, not a whole lot of movement in the share price is seen. When the lines start to move apart from one another, it's typical to see some sort of movement, higher or lower, in the share price.

Bollinger Bands.

This is an interesting tool to use while trading, and looking for companies that might be on the verge of a move higher. When used in your active chart during day trading, the Bollinger bands seems to expand and move apart from each other at times, and compress and grow closer together as the spread between the bid and ask gets tighter. Just as I refer to RSI indicators to see if the share price is currently considered overbought, or over sold, the Bollinger bands are also useful for determining when to buy and sell. As a general rule, when the share price touches, or breaks through, the top Bollinger band, you might want to consider that as a sell signal. When it touches, or falls below the lower Bollinger band, you might want to consider buying. When analyzing stocks to swing trade you should also use Bollinger bands to look for the same indicators. On exceptionally volatile and dynamic days in the market, if the share price has been trending higher, the Bollinger bands moving closer together in a very tight trading range and can be very predictive of an impending move in the direction of the overall daily trend.

The price to play the game.

My middle son likens the level of players playing Stock Market Baseball to A, AA, AAA, and Major League levels, as well as the difference between Major markets, and Small Market teams, but for the time being I'm just going to focus on the practical costs of playing Stock Market Baseball and what you might expect to make, percentage wise, if your trades go well, based on what you're able to invest.

Anybody can play Stock Market Baseball, whether they are actually investing real money, or just using practice accounts. I know that the trading platform thinkorswim®, a TDAmeritrade, Inc. [i] related company, allows folks to test out their trading theories and ideas in a format that does not actually require hard dollar investments. I'm sure that other companies like Charles Schwab [ii], and Etrade [iii], probably offer a similar service. For hard cost illustrations, as to what the payback could be from using Stock Market Baseball, as a basis for your approach to trading stocks, let me illustrate what different levels of investment could return, if you suffered no losses.

First of all, I do not suggest playing Stock Market Baseball using actual dollars to trade with to anyone that cannot risk $5000 to trade. Why? Primarily because the amount that you can make, in relationship to the amount of fees and taxes that you would have to pay on your gain, might make trading in stocks too economically risky, and financially unrewarding. Take, for example someone using $2000 to trade with . 1% of 2000 is $20.00 But you would have to pay about $20, in the case of TDAmeritrade, Inc. to buy and sell that trade. So, for the risk of the trade, and a 1% return, all you would have to show for that trade would be nothing, zero, nada, zilch. But you could also lose. Not worth the risk, in my opinion. At $5000, the odds change a little more in your favor. 1% of $5000 is $50.00. Deduct $20 for the buying and the selling fees from TDAmeritrade, Inc. and you end up with $30.00 on a 1% return for the day, $150.00 for the week, and $600,00 for the month. That's not enough to live on, but it might be enough to pay for groceries, to pay for rent, or to pay for a car payment. In a two income family, where one person is a stay at home mom, or dad, that extra $600.00 a month could really come in handy. 1% on $10,000 traded, not counting trading fees and short term capital gains taxes, would make you $100.00 a day , $500.00 a week, about $2000 a month, and $24,000 a year. Not a bad income for someone coming out of college, or with a limited amount to trade with .

The dollar amount that most online brokerages want to see, and that opens up more possibilities to you, in the form of trading on margin, is about $25,000. 00. Think about this. 1 % of $25,000.00 is $250.00, $1250 per week, $5000 a month, and $60,000.00 a year. That's a better income level than most teachers, store managers, and small business owners with a couple of employees, makes. And you can make this on a 1% a day gain, on $25,000.00 traded, using a Stock Market Baseball approach. You don't have to swing for the bleachers, in order to make money in the stock market. All you need to do is find stocks that are moving, one way, or the other, and jump on for a small, or large, percentage of the rise, or fall, in share price. 1%, or 2% a day, is doable. Once again, pay attention to what I wrote earlier about the amount you can afford to risk. If you can't afford to risk your entire investment in the stock market, don't play the Stock Market Baseball game, or trade the markets. Because, even though I'm trying to present a way to manage risk by focusing on 1%, 2%, and 3% average returns a day, you can still lose money on trades that don't go your way.

Stock Market Baseball Scorecard.

How can you know if you're winning the game of Stock Market Baseball unless you're able to keep score? Keep a Stock Market Baseball scorecard to use from week to week. Every week is equal to a game. Since there are five days in a week, every day of the week equals an inning and how your team did that day. Consequently, there are 5 innings in a game of Stock Market Baseball. Since there are 52 weeks in a year, there would also be 52 weekly games in a season of Stock Market Baseball. You don't have to wait for January to start playing Stock Market Baseball. You can start playing, and trading, at anytime of the year.

Think of your stocks as your players, with you as your team's manager, picking players, and managing moves, against your adversaries, the market makers, or other traders. Market makers know how they're going to effect the trading of the stock better than you do, much like a pitcher knowing what he's going to pitch before you see it coming at you. But you don't have to hit a home run to win Stock Market Baseball. You just need to get on base, and score a run a week. You do that, and you'll win the weekly game, the monthly game, and the overall season, and get paid accordingly. If you can score more runs, or gain more percentage returns on your investments, so much the better.

By the end of each month, or year, you can also keep track of which days of the week seemed to have been the best days for you to make percentage gains in the market. Keep record of the companies whose shares you had the most success trading. Just like hitters get to know pitchers tendencies, you might find some market makers whose moves you've been able to predict with some consistency. If you find yourself swing trading a company for a few days, or weeks, rather than day trading, just average your percentage gains over how many days, or weeks that you were in your position, and enter the average daily percentage return into the appropriate daily, and weekly scorecard.

At the end of the year, or 52 week period of time, or shorter period of time that you decide to trade and play the game, calculate your weekly gains and losses, by the day, week, and 52 week season. See how you did. See what days of the week, or innings, were better for you than others. See what weeks, and months of the year, were better for you than others. Keep track of what players, (your stock picks), paid off for you better than others, and if there were certain sectors that performed for you better than others. Learn from the data, and your experiences. Use that information and experience to get prepared for the new Stock Market Baseball season to come.

Using percentage numbers, what was your total annual percentage gain on Monday? Tuesday? Wednesday? Thursday. And Friday? What day of the week was best for you? What months of the year were better than others for you? Which months were worse? What stocks seemed to make money for you? What sectors did they come from? What chart patterns and technical tools did you use to find them? All of this information can be helpful to you as you make your future plans and preparations. Remember, you're the manager of your team, or investments. You're the one that is going to make the decisions as to what moves you're going to make to win your games, and season. 1% a day is all you need to perform well. Anything above that is gravy, and can only benefit you.

One percent a day

©2013 John George Campbell   stockmarketbaseball.com

One percent a day

By this time you should have gotten the message that I think that you can make a lot of money by the end of the year just by gaining 1% a day, on average, on your investment. But if it was that easy, than everybody would be doing it. Mutual fund and institutional fund managers would be doing it, but most aren't. Most can't. Most don't even exceed 10% a year on funds under management. Not because they don't know how to invest, and trade. They're professionals. This is something they do for a living, but they are too big. And most fund managers, with the exception of hedge fund managers, are precluded from having more than 5% of their total portfolio invested in any one stock. If they tried to enter a lower priced, lightly traded stock, with a million dollar investment, with the objective of buying and selling, in the same day, their entry into the stock would cause a huge spike, probably above what they would want to pay, and their exit would cause a huge collapse of the share price, if they could find a buyer. So, they, by virtue of their size, are too large to play stock market baseball on lower priced, lightly traded stocks. But the individual trader isn't.

The individual trader is more mobile and nimble, more able to make quick changes, to get in and get out quickly, since their buys and sells will hardly make a ripple in the overall volatility of the stock to be traded.

Another advantage for the individual trader versus the fund manager is the size of investment dollars managed. Many fund managers manage hundreds of millions, if not billions, of dollars. As mentioned before, due to internal risk management controls at their firms, many are precluded from investing more than 5% of their entire portfolio in just one investment, unless they happen to be hedge fund managers, or private equity companies. But the individual investor isn't bound by these size constraints, or risk management requirements.

You, as the individual trader, can choose to trade 100% of your trading account on one investment. You can choose to trade stocks with a share price value of less than $5.00 a share. You can also experience a greater percentage of your investment losing, or making, money, depending how much of your trading account that you're trading with. Because of their sheer size it has to be a lot harder for large funds to return much more than 10%, 20%, 30%, 40%, or 50%, per year, over the course of several years. Some, don't even return 10% on money invested with their funds, per year, over several years time. But you, as a small individual investor, and trader, can generate better than 100% return on your investments per year, over several years. Simply because you aren't bound by the same risk management parameters that the big boys are bound by.

That doesn't mean that Stock Market Baseball can't be played by the bigger players with deeper pockets. It just means that they need to play their game with stocks that have a higher share price, and more average daily volume, so that their buys and sells don't make as big of a splash, and expose their play. Unless they want it to.

One of the many reasons why people are attracted to the stock market, and also afraid of the stock market, is the massive amounts of money that can be made and lost in the stock market. Everybody likes to hear about some lucky trader, or investor, that made a killing in the markets, and became a millionaire, or billionaire, overnight. They like to see these home runs, and wish they could hit home runs too.

But the reality of the situation is that, for the typical investor,

Stock Market Baseball is won by getting on the bases, and moving your runners, your investments, into scoring position, and across home plate. And that's easier to do hitting the ball safely into the field of play, and making 1%, 2%, and 3% on your investments, day in, and day out. Every now and then you will find a stock that makes you 5%, 10%, 20% in a day, or week.

You'll enter the trade, and all of a sudden your up 5% on positive news. Other players start jumping on to catch that stocks momentum, and now you're up 10%. From learning to read charts, and understanding Fibonacci levels, and areas of support and resistance, you can tell that the stock has a little more ways to run before it tests resistance. So you let your winner run another day, or two, or week, or two, and maybe squeeze another 5% to 10% out of that run. If your initial goal was just to make 1% or 2% a day, this extra 10% to 20% gain is like a few back-to-back home runs. They don't happen all the time, but when they do, maximize the opportunity, but don't blow the play. Don't try to time the top of the move. Get out with your profit before the rally, or run, is over, and get prepared for your next play.

Potential Daily, Weekly, and Annual returns making 1%, 2%, or 3% a day

To give you an idea of what 1% , 2%, or 3% a day can do for your daily, weekly, and annual return on investment, I've made a few tables. Try to remember to not get greedy. Stocks move up, and down. The market maker's job is to make a market for the shares of the stock that he's trading. He can't do that by simply taking the share price in just one direction. There will be reversals. Keep aware of this, and if you're real good, you might be able to make money following the moves, up, and down, long, or short.

The following tables are posted in a larger size at http://stockmarketbaseball.com .

Daily return on investment, based on amount invested, and % returned on that investment, per week.

Daily return on investment, based on amount invested, and percentage returned on that investment, per day.

Investment	1%	2%	3%
$5000	50	100	150
$10000	100	200	300
$15000	150	300	450
$20000	200	400	600
$25000	250	500	750
$30000	300	600	900
$35000	350	700	1050
$40000	400	800	1200
$45000	450	900	1350
$50000	500	1000	1500

© October, 2013 John George Campbell, Stock Market Baseball
(The numbers shown above are possible daily returns, considering no losses, before fees and state and federal taxes are accounted for. There is no guarantee that anyone trading stocks will consistently make these gains. People can, and do, lose money, trading in the stock market. The table just shows you what is possible.)

Weekly return on investment, based on amount invested, and % returned on that investment, per week.

Weekly return on investment, based on amount invested, and percentage returned on that investment, per day.

Investment	1%	2%	3%
$5000	250	500	750
$10000	500	1000	1500
$15000	750	1500	2250
$20000	1000	2000	3000
$25000	1250	2500	3750
$30000	1500	3000	4500
$35000	1750	3500	5250
$40000	2000	4000	6000
$45000	2250	4500	6750
$50000	2500	5000	7500

© October, 2013 John George Campbell, Stock Market Baseball
(The numbers shown above are possible weekly returns, considering no losses, before fees and state and federal taxes are accounted for. There is no guarantee that anyone trading stocks will consistently make these gains. People can, and do, lose money, trading in the stock market. The table just shows you what is possible.)

Annual return on investment, based on the amount invested, and the percentage returned on that investment, per day.

Annual return on investment, based on amount invested, and percentage returned on that investment, per day.

Investment	1%	2%	3%
$5000	13000	26000	39000
$10000	26000	52000	78000
$15000	39000	78000	117000
$20000	52000	104000	156000
$25000	65000	13000	195000
$30000	78000	156000	234000
$35000	91000	182000	273000
$40000	104000	208000	312000
$45000	117000	234000	351000
$50000	130000	260000	390000

© 2013 John George Campbell, Stock Market Baseball

© October, 2013 John George Campbell, Stock Market Baseball
(The numbers shown above are possible annual returns, considering no losses, before fees and state and federal taxes are accounted for. There is no guarantee that anyone trading stocks will consistently make these gains. People can, and do, lose money, trading in the stock market. The table just shows you what is possible.)

One other thing to keep in mind, is that if your investments are earning returns every day, your actual payback at the end of the year could be greater than what I've indicated on my tables, because each day you would have just a bit more in your trading account to trade with, when you add in the gains made each day to the amount you initially traded with. Sort of like compound interest.

"They told me that there would be no math !" Chevy Chase, impersonating President Gerald Ford, Saturday Night Live, NBC, 1975. [iv]

I know that most people could do the simple math to arrive at the daily, weekly, and annual returns, based on amounts invested and percentages gained, but since I'm the one writing the book, I thought I'd save you some time and do it for you. However, just because you now have tables showing you what gains are possible, that doesn't mean that you will achieve these results. Some days you'll exceed 1%, 2%, or 3% in gains. Some days you won't even make 1%. Some days you'll lose money, and see a percentage loss. Some days you'll decide to stay in the trade overnight, because you want to ride the momentum of a winning stock pick, in order to maximize your gain. That's OK to do, as long as you define what your exit strategy is, and get out of the trade when you've reached your target, or when the trade starts to diminish your gain.

There is something else that I want you to consider about the weekly, and 52 week, tables. Think about how much you make in a week, a month, or a year. How do the numbers in the weekly, and 52 week annual return table compare to what you're currently making?

How do they compare to what some of the small businessmen

and women in your community make? Remember that these independent business people invest their money in their businesses hoping, budgeting, and planning for a certain return on their investment. I've owned a couple of small businesses. One where I've had several employees working for me. One for which I was my only employee. Ironically, I made more money with less overhead, less management oversight, less government red tape, when I worked for myself, with no employees. You don't have the repartee, and camaraderie, and social interaction when you work solely for yourself. You're also on the hook for all of the financial risk, and reward, when you work for yourself. But it is quite personally satisfying to act on your own ideas and see them develop and become financially, and experientially, rewarding. You can achieve that kind of independence and personal growth and prosperity through learning to trade stocks, and at the same time earn as much, or more, than many small business owners in your area, on your investment in the financial markets, if you can approach the markets with realistic daily, weekly, and monthly, and annual expectations.

That's where an exercise, and game, like Stock Market Baseball comes in. It doesn't require you to make 5%, 10%, 20%, 50%, or 100% on your money in a day, week, or month. It just helps you to target the very possible returns on your investment of 1%, 2%, or 3% a day. If you are able to stay disciplined, and keep clearly defined targets for entering a trade, and exiting a trade, you will have taken some wise steps to prudently approach making money in the stock market without needing to ever hit the ball out of the park . Think small ball. Think singles and doubles. With them you stand a much better chance of winning the game. You'll hit a home run, every now and then, but hitting singles and doubles, for 1% and 2% gains on your investment, daily, will be much easier to do consistently.

One more thing. You may think, from reading what I've written, that I'm a day trader, trading the markets, every day. Making percentage gains, every day. That's not the case. I'm more of a swing trader, than a day trader. I usually enter a trade, and hold onto it for a few weeks, or months, until my target price, or percentage gain, is achieved. I like to take a position in a stock that I see is on the move, and maximize my gain, over a certain period of time. I then divide my overall gain by the days that I've been invested in the stock traded. In this way I can reduce trading fees, and daily stress from needing to trade daily, all the while giving the trade maximum opportunity to return the highest gain for me. If my way of trading works for you, than good. If you need to trade daily, and don't mind the extra stress and trading fees, than have at it. I guess I'm more of a low stress kind of guy, and I like it that way.

When to hit the long ball, and go for extra bases.

There are many occasions, when targeting a return greater than 1%, or 2%, makes sense. When you get used to reading stock charts and understand technical indicators like Fibonacci ladders, support and resistance levels, Bollinger bands, the Relative Strength Index, Stochastics, and MACD, and you can see, from just looking at the chart that the share price has 5% or 10% or 20% more to go before reaching it's next level of support, or resistance, that you might want to forego the day trading strategy, and focus more on a swing trading strategy, and stay in the investment a few more days, or even a couple of weeks.

When I first started focusing on making 1% or 2% a day I knew from past experiences that stocks can break out on runs, or rallies, that last from a few days to a few weeks, or months, in duration. In that time period a stock's share price might rise 10% to 50%, or more. When my research and analysis seem to indicate that a stock is in this rally mode, I find it best to let your winners run, in order to maximize your percentage gain. But in this situation, when you look back at it, if you've made 10% in a week, or 20% over 2 weeks, you've actually averaged 2% a day, haven't you? It's just an extended version of arriving at the daily goal, without making daily trades to achieve the goal. In a situation like this, you become more of your own personal equity manager, monitoring your investment, rather than trading it every day. Your trading fees pertaining to this kind of swing trade are less, since you aren't trading in and out every day. In truth, this is how I prefer to trade. I like swing trading better than day trading, mostly for the reduced daily stress, the lower cumulative trading fees, and the ability to monitor other trades without the need to track one specific investment every minute of the trading day.

Here's an example of a swing trade where I averaged 3% a day, over three days. I bought 2200 shares of ZION for $10.77 and $10.78 on April 21st, 2009. Three days later, on April 24th, I sold all 2200 shares for $11.80 a share. That was better than a 9% return on my investment within 3 days, or an average of better than 3% a day, for each of those three days.

Another trade that I made right before the Zion trade was for 10.000 shares of C (Citigroup) on March 23rd, 2009 for $3.05 a share. I sold the 10,000 shares of Citigroup, 17 trading days later, on April 17th, 2009 for $3.67 a share. That represented a 20% gain over 17 trading days, or 1.176 % per day over that time period. Another reason why I'm showing this trade to you is to show that with swing trading you don't have to be right on the day that you enter a trade to ultimately make money on the trade. From the chart pattern leading up to my buy, it looked as though Citigroup was on a trend higher. So I entered the trade. Within the next few days, Citigroup pulled back on some profit taking, but ultimately ended up higher than my entry point. You can also see from that trade that I held onto the trade maybe a day too long, as I could have made more profit by selling on the 14th, or the 16th, but I still made money on the trade, and better than the 1% a day that's been my stated goal.

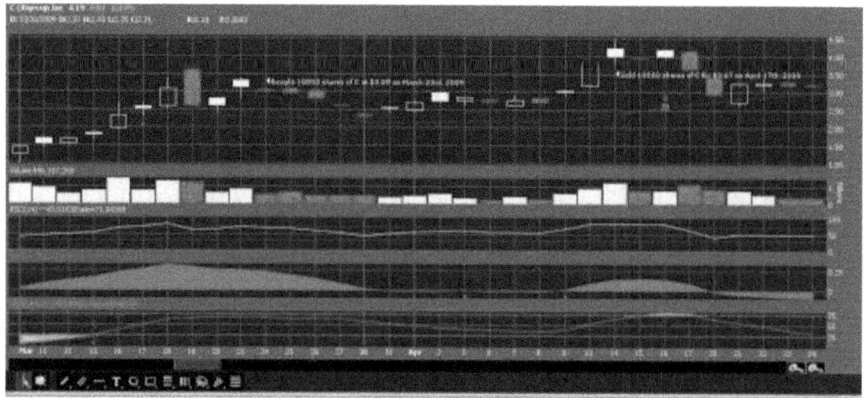

thinkorswim® ProphetCharts® v

You can see from the trading history pertaining to the ZION and C trades that I've just described, that it's not only possible to make 1% to 3% a day in the stock market, on average. It's doable.

Here's a more recent analysis that I did in October, 2013, while writing an article about Capstone Turbine. I hadn't focused much attention to it before, but immediately saw, by looking at Fibonacci levels that Capstone, CPST, was bouncing off support at $1.17. I predicted that if it bounced off support at $1.17 that it might be a good time to buy shares. Six days after I wrote the article the price was at $1.28. I didn't need to do a time consuming fundamental analysis of everything that made Capstone work as a trade. The chart told me in a few minutes all I needed to know.

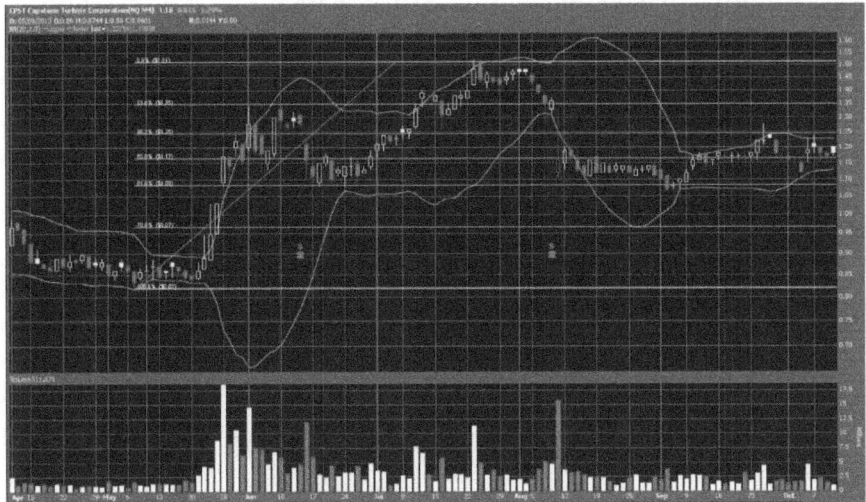

thinkorswim® ProphetCharts® vi

The BIG Grand Slam

The more you play the game of Stock Market Baseball, the better you'll be able recognize certain chart patterns that are suggestive of impending breakouts. Here are a few patterns that I look for.

The Golden Cross

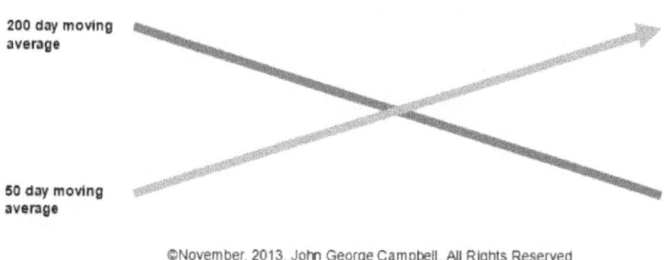

©November, 2013, John George Campbell. All Rights Reserved.

The Golden Cross

This Golden Cross pattern is one of my favorite patterns to review since, for me, it signals something very significant happening with the share price. While it's really not considered a chart pattern, it's moving average indicators get my serious focus and attention. The 50 day moving average, reflecting moderate to recent share price direction in the stock, is breaking through a long term point of resistance for the share price, the 200 day moving average. So the chart is telling you a story that, many times, hasn't been printed in words yet. In simple terms, the share price, as reflected in the 50 day moving average, hasn't been able to rise above the 200 day moving average for over 6 months. But, now it is. Why? Why is the share price able to break through a price barrier that it hasn't been able to break through for more than six months? That's really a big deal. And sometimes you won't find any press releases to tell you what the chart is telling you, graphically. So, believe your eyes, and do some more research on the stocks whose charts are showing you a Golden Cross.

Cup and Handle

© November 2013, John George Campbell. All Rights Reserved.

Cup and Handle

The Cup and Handle has been a favorite chart pattern for many longs looking for a stock that may break higher. On the far left side of the pattern is a deep decline in share price, creating the left side of the cup. Perhaps the company had bad news back then, or issued more shares, thus causing a dilutive effect on the share price. If you're a real good detective you'll probably do the research to find out what happened back then, but for our purposes, you just have to note that deep decline forming the left side of the cup. Then, over many weeks, months, and sometimes, years, the stock price languishes in a sort of horizontal direction. Not moving noticeably higher, or lower. Subsequently, something happens, known, or unknown, published in the press, or not, that causes the share price to rise. In a relatively short period of time, whether that be days, weeks, or months, the share price has risen in such a way that the right side of the pattern now looks like the right side of a cup. The bottom of the pattern looks like the bottom of the cup, and the left side looks like the left side of the cup. But the pattern isn't complete yet. Once the share price has reached a level, on the right side of the cup, that's similar to where it had been trading on the left side of the cup, before the share price plummeted, the share price once again starts to move in a horizontal pattern, but with momentary and slight declines in the share price. This horizontal move to the right side of the top of the cup may take a few weeks, or months to fully form, but it's during this period of time when new longs to this investment might want to buy shares. And then wait. Buy and hold. But don't just buy in just because the chart pattern has been formed. Buy in when you've done some due diligence on the company, know what they do, how they're managed, how many shares they have outstanding, how many shares in the float, how many shares actually get traded everyday, on average, How many shares are owned by insiders, what percentage of shares are owned by institutions, what percentage of shares are short the stock, etc... If you want to score big, it will take quite a bit more work, research, and patience to find the right investment, understand the investment, and go through some market maker volatility games before you might score.

Inverted Head and Shoulders

© November 2013, John George Campbell. All Rights Reserved.

Inverted Head and Shoulders

The Inverted Head and Shoulders chart formation also takes a little time to develop. After a decline in the share price on the left side of the chart, the share price rallies on an angular direction to test some higher level of resistance, sometimes equal to the price it had originally fallen from on the left side of the pattern, but the rally fails, and the share price declines, again on an angular direction, until it finds support at a lower level, just below the support level it had initially rallied from. Then, once again, the share price starts to rally to the previous resistance level that it had failed to rise above before. And it fails again, and slowly sells off in an angular direction, once again to test the bottom level of support. But this time, as it rebounds off the lower support level, it rallies higher to the point of resistance that it has failed to rise above, at least two times before, but this time it takes out that resistance level, and with no immediate resistance above the share price moves quickly to a higher trading range, quite a few percentage points higher. Maybe 10% to 50% to 100% higher than the recent level of resistance that had been so hard to break through. So, the way to play the reverse upside down head and shoulders, if you don't want to wait for the whole pattern to develop, is to try to recognize the completion of the pattern right before it tests the higher point of resistance for the last time.

Reverse Gap Up

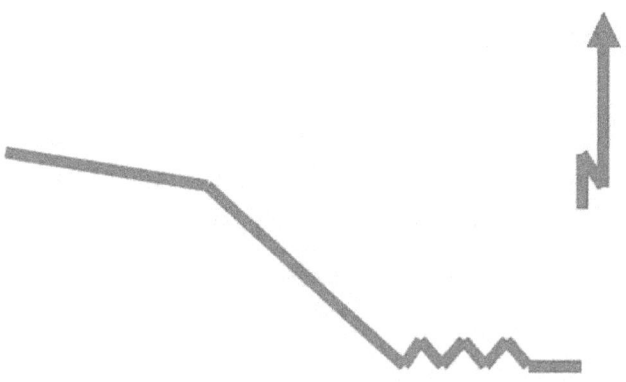

© November 2013, John George Campbell. All Rghts Reserved.

Reverse Gap up

The reason why this Reverse Gap Up chart pattern gets my attention, is because it usually signifies something very significant going on behind the scenes, that would cause the share price to gap up from a very depressed price level. Sometimes the reason for the gap up are made clear, through press releases pertaining to an important event for the company. Sometimes these gap ups happen completely in the absence of any news at all. Personally, I prefer the chart where the gap up occurs on no news, since to me, it means that the powers that be, behind the scenes, want to keep a lid on the news that will effect a continuing increase in share price. That may also mean that they want to continue to accumulate shares before any significant news, pertaining to the stock, is released. I would want to get into this stock before they actually release the news that will take the share price higher.

In the game of Stock Market Baseball, playing for home runs isn't the same as playing for singles, or doubles. I can find single, or doubles, just by focusing on short term technical indicators, like the 50 day moving average crossing the 200 day moving average, or the 12 day crossing the 26 day moving average, or RSI bought and oversold indicators, or momentum based on positive, or negative press releases, but finding and playing for a multi-bag grand slam home run takes more time, research, and patience to let the investment pay off. But they can pay off very big, as my experience with HGSI , in 2009, will show.

HGSI Grand Slam Play by Play

In order to find HGSI I decided to test a Reverse Gap Up chart. My thought was that if a company, whose stock's share price had previously tanked, or dropped, below a dollar, could all of a sudden gap up in share price from 88 cents to the $1.30 level, on very large volume, then there must be something going on behind the scenes to drive that kind of change in share price, change in trend direction,and increase in volume. So I bought 19000 shares at $1.32 and let the momentum take me where it wanted to go. In this case into the low $2's, where I sold 2000 shares for $2.20, and 17,000 shares for $2.17, and then went short in the low $2's for another 3% gain, before going long again.

Before going into more of the HGSI trading experience I want to review the first trade, where I bought 19,000 shares for $1.32 a share, and sold 2000 shares for $2.20 a share, and 17000 shares for $2.17 a share. That entire trade, from the buy, to the sell, took just 10 days. I made a 67% gain in 10 days on the sale at $2.20 , and a 66% gain in 10 days on the sale at $2.17. Or 6.7% a day, and 6.6% a day, return on my investment when using the Stock Market Baseball score card. Then I shorted shares at $2.02, and $2.00, on May 4th, 2009, and then covered those short trades at $1.94, and $1.9499, on May 5th, 2009 for an approximate 3% gain in two days. Or 1.5% a day. Then I went long again.

Something to note, for those of you inclined to analyze things further, notice that after I entered my initial trade at $1.32, that the share price dipped below $1.30 for a couple of days. In my opinion, that was to be expected, after the gap up it had just experienced. Even my buy at $1.32 had been on one of those declining days in the chart, so I was taking advantage of the pullback to buy shares myself. So, for those of you that make a move on a stock following a gap up, don't immediately exit your trade because the trade moves a few pennies, or percentage points, against you. Understand the nature of the market, and the market maker, and just plain stock market physics. Something that goes up will come down. Stocks that experience sudden spikes will start to pullback after the spike. If your other technical indicators suggest to you that this is still a good trade, then trust your experience, and with respect to the ladies, your investment intuition. I had been in these situations before, and trusted my experience to wait things out, and it wasn't long at all, within 10 days, that the initial trade paid off very well.

After having completed my successful initial trades in HGSI, one long, and one short, I bought more shares. Believing that upward momentum had just got started, I bought 7700 shares of HGSI between $1.94 and $1.9499, on May 5th, 2009. I added 13,513 shares on May 6th, 2009, at $2.25. I had a new position in HGSI of 21,213 shares. And here's where the story get's interesting. By June 4th HGSI had closed at $3.15, and that wasn't even the high for that day. But did I sell ? No. I was greedy, and thought that the share price had just entered a new range that I wanted to see solidify. But the share price pulled back into the lower 2's, just above my last buy price at $2.25. I thought it would rebound, and then I would cash out. And it did that. The share price rebounded to $3.00, on July 1st. But did I sell? Nope. Greed again. I thought that once it reached $3.00 again that it would break through upper resistance and enter into this higher trading range that I was expecting. I was wrong, and played it wrong, and I grew just a little disgusted with myself as the share price pulled back to the $2.30 range, where, in fear, and discouraged, I sold 16,736 shares for $2.30 a share, and 4477 shares for $2.26 a share, on July 8th.

By the next day, I began to think that I had made a mistake in selling. That next day the share price hadn't risen much, but it was higher than what I had sold at. I could see from the lack of volume selling, that the bottom of the recent moved had been reached on the day that I had sold, and since my sell prices had all been above my previous buying prices, I knew that I wasn't going to have any problems with IRS wash sale rules, from buying HGSI again, even if it was for a higher price than what I had just sold at the day before. So, on July 9th, 2009 I re-entered a position in HGSI with 20,000 shares at $2.45, and 5,000 shares at $2.50. I had realized that I had just been fooled by the big bad Market Maker the day before, and even though I was personally, and very privately embarrassed about that, I wasn't too proud to recognize my mistake, and get back into my position with HGSI, even increasing my position by a few thousand shares.

By the week of July 13th, 2009 the average daily volume for HGSI had started to increase from about 2.5 million shares a day, to 3.6 million shares traded on both Monday, the 13th, and Tuesday, the 14th, to 7.9 million shares traded on Wednesday July 15th. And the price on Wednesday had increased by 10% from $2.50 to $2.75, on more than 3 times the average daily volume. Something was definitely up. Money, and volume, was rushing into HGSI. On Thursday, July 16th, the share price closed at $3.35 on over 39 million shares traded, for a better than 30% increase in share price from the beginning of the week, on greater than 15x's the average daily volume. Friday would be the day to find out if this move was going to carry on through the next week, or sell-off, as day traders, and momentum traders, took their profits.

Friday started off a little higher than Thursday's close at $3.35. Day traders, swing traders, and momentum traders did take profits that day, but the share price remained strong, just closing 1% lower, at $3.32, on persistent heavy volume of 26 million shares. All of this huge weekly move in share price, and volume, occurred on no news.

On Monday, July 20th, HGSI opened above $10.00 on positive news released about it's drug to treat Lupus, Benlysta, and closed above $12.50. On Friday, July 24th, HGSI closed the first week, after Monday's initial price spike, at $14.64. By July 31st, HGSI had given up a few percent to close the month of July out at $14.30.

My move to increase my position of HGSI by a few thousand shares had paid off, BIG, even though I had paid a few percent more than what I had just sold HGSI for, just the day before.

I bring this up to address a common situation that most folks that invest and trade in the markets go through. Self-doubt, discouragement, fear, sometimes, and disgust for being so stupid to not make the right trading decisions. Well, GET OVER IT.

Everyone that trades the markets makes bad decisions from time to time. Learn from your mistakes, and if they aren't big ones, and you can get back into the game, do so as analytically, and resolutely, and as soon, as possible. Analyze your mistakes. Determine your options. Trust your instincts, and experience. Dust yourself off. And get back in the game. If you can't deal with adversity, whether a lot, or a little, you might not be of the right temperament, or maturity to invest, trade, and yes, play, the markets. If you can't develop some backbone to internally support your decisions, and you're always whining about everything that you perceive that's going wrong, and can't develop any patience with respect to your investments, then you probably aren't the right kind of person to personally trade the markets, or personally manage your investments. In that case, have someone that does have the experience, and personal qualities that are needed, to manage and invest for you. There are many professionally trained, and seasoned, traders, stock brokers, fund managers, and hedge fund managers that have the experience and know how to get the job done for you. But if you want to do these things for yourself, then continue to read books like this one, visit online investment sites focusing on technical analysis, and investment advice, and attend investment seminars, where you can learn the things that you need to know to help you become successful at trading and the game of Stock Market Baseball.

Keeping score. By July 17th, my HGSI buys at $2.50, on July 9th had increased over 32%, in just over a weeks time. By that following Monday, July 20th, 2009, that $2.50 per share buy had increased over 500% per share, in 8 trading days . By the end of the month of July, on July 31st, 2009, that $2.50 per share of HGSI had increased 573%, to close the month out at $14.30.

Still, you can't count as a win, that which you haven't cashed out and accounted for. What I ended up doing was selling 2,485 shares at $14.03, 2,500 shares at $13.63, and 2,500 shares for $13.58, all on July 27th, 2009. 5,000 of these shares were sold in the after hours session, when the share priced looked like it was about to tank below $13.00. In that case, I definitely reacted to what I was seeing with a little bit of fear, a little bit of greed, in protecting some profits, and a lot of financial necessity, since I needed the money, and HGSI had already completely surpassed what my original exit target was, when it completely bypassed the mid 7 dollar range and spiked up to the 12's on Monday, July 20th. So, as far as I was concerned, I had all sorts of a cushion to practice a little patience with, but I didn't want to be foolish and watch all the gains disappear either. So, I sold some shares on the the 27th of July. And I still had better than 17500 HGSI shares left, unsold.

Getting back to keeping score again, I made better than 560% on the actual shares sold at $14.03. Better than 545% on the shares sold at $13.63, and better than 543% on the shares sold at $13.58. All within the month of July, 2009, 20 days after buying the shares.

Breaking that down on the scoreboard I would divide the 560% gain by the number of trading days between July 9th, and July 27th, which in this case, was 16 trading days, for a percentage gain per each trading day of 35 %. Remember. I didn't sell any shares between July 9th and July 26th, until my sale of shares on the 27th. So the overall gain needs to be divided by the number of days between the buying and selling of the shares to arrive at an average percentage return per day. Still, not too shabby. Gaining 35% in a month would be a great month. 35% a day for 16 days definitely had put a nice hitch in my git-a-long. I would do the same division exercise with the shares sold for 545% and 543% gains.

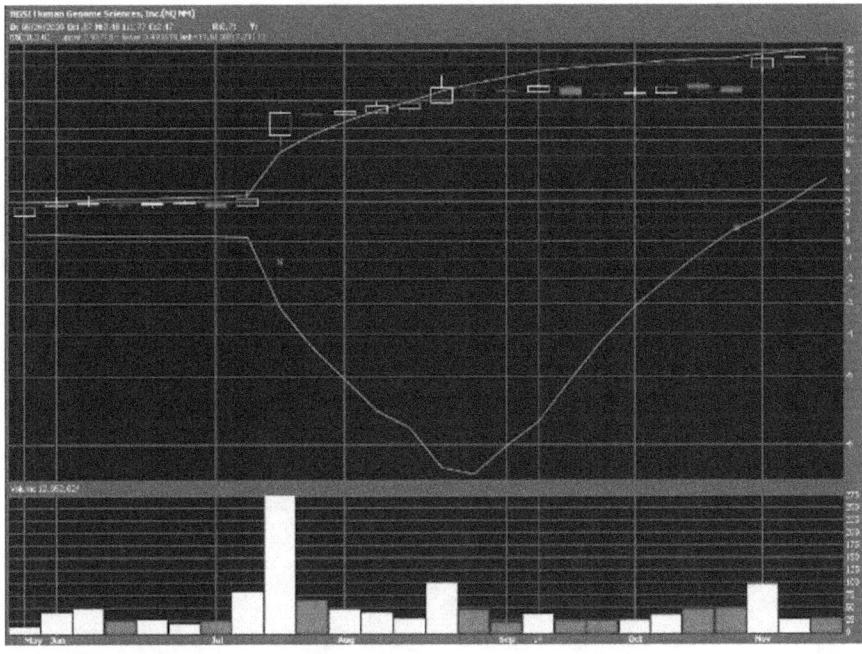

thinkorswim® ProphetCharts® vii

The HGSI chart above, from 2009, shows the move from the low $1.00 range in May , 2009, to $29.00 by November and December, 2009. Notice how the OBV, On Balance Volume tripled from May to June, and then increased by several hundred percent in July, right before HGSI, Human Genome Sciences, Incorporated, gapped to $10.50, on a Monday, after having closed around $3.25 the Friday before..

Both increases in OBV in May, and July, 2009 were strong technical indicators of money flowing to HGSI, in advance of the 300% move higher in share price that Monday in July 2009. The increase in volume, truly preceded the increase in share price. Something else to pay attention to is the drop off in volume when the share priced reached $29.00. I took that as a signal to sell my remaining shares. Even though the share price did move into the $30 range for a brief time, the share price soon started to fall below the price I sold at, and just kept falling. Once again , the decrease in OBV, signaled a lack of buying interest in HGSI at that price level, and so it was a good time to sell.

But the markets STINK !!!! So, go short !

Yeah ?

So ?

Does the market's stinking and moving lower mean that you can't make money on the market's trend lower? Of course not. Do what, in my opinion, most Hedge Fund managers, and professional traders do, in that situation.

Go short.

When the markets are going lower, based on your technical analysis, and not what talking heads on TV, or the internet say, then do your research to find stocks that are showing signs of dropping lower in price. Remember. They don't have to drop a lot to make you money. Just 1%, or 2%, a day. And that's very doable. You can find them. You can make money on their moves lower. You can profit from a trend in share price that you had nothing to do with in creating, or sustaining. Their share price is going lower, and you are just going along for the ride, much the same way you would when you used to be a kid on a swing. One moment the swing would take you higher. The next moment the swing would take you lower. But, as a kid, what did you care? All you cared about was the fun you were having riding the swing. Look at trading the shares of stocks in the same manner. Enjoy the ride up, and enjoy the ride down. And enjoy the fun you'll have making a profit in either direction.

On January 29th, 2009 I shorted 3000 shares of TXT at $9.07. I covered that short trade about 2 hours later at $8.94 a share for about a 1.5 % gain in less than 2 hours. For the reader that doesn't know what going short, or shorting, is, it's the process of borrowing a number of shares from a broker, at a certain price, say $10.00 a share, and selling those shares short, meaning that you're speculating, or projecting, that the share price is going lower than the price that you borrowed them at. When the share price hit's your target price below $10.00, say, $9.50, you then buy to cover your short position. The borrowed shares are returned to the broker, and you make the difference between the price that you borrowed the shares at, in this case $10.00, and what you paid to cover those short shares at, in this case $9.50. Your profit on this transaction would be 50 cents a share, minus trading fees, and whatever fee the broker might charge for letting you borrow their shares.

Why would you short any stock? Isn't that Un-American, economically evil, and a dastardly thing to do? No. Contrary to popular opinion, shorting stocks that are trending lower doesn't have any inherent lack of virtue, at all. It's just a financial judgment on your part that the share price for a stock is going to go lower than the price a broker will allow you to borrow shares from them at. Think back once again to my previous kid's swing analogy. The swing goes up. The swing goes down. So do share prices, on any given day. Even on bullish days, when the share price is breaking higher, there will be many moments in the day where the share price of that bullish stock pulls back a bit. Share prices never go straight up, or straight down, without eventually moving in the other direction, as well. Try to profit from these moves.

During the week that I shorted TXT, I also successfully shorted ALL, and GNW. I didn't make one long trade that entire week. Why? Probably because in the beginning of 2009, with a new presidential administration in the Whitehouse, a balance of power shift in congress, and the American financial system in a very threatening mess, as well as political wrangling over helping,or not helping, the American car industry, the markets were in a lot of turmoil, and many company's share prices were trending lower. So, rather than complain about the direction of the market, and cry "WOE IS ME ! WOE IS ME !", I thought it best to take the sour lemon stories that the news was reporting and make lemonade. In baseball terms, I just took what the markets were giving me. In baseball, if the infield has shifted towards third base, because they expect the batter to hit to that side, if I'm the batter, and I can hit to the opposite field, safely, I'm going to take the advice of the early baseball hitting great, Wee Willie Keeler, and "hit them where they ain't". If you can't make money going long on stocks, then take what's given to you, and make money going short.

But I'm not rich ! I can't afford to play the game !

I've been trading stocks for a number of years now, but before 2009 it had always been a very limited involvement, though, many years, the money I made from trading stocks represented the largest part of my annual income. But with the economy in a shambles in 2007 and 2008, finding a job, and making a living wage, was getting to be exceedingly hard to do. In fact, for me and my family, we were getting awfully close to defaulting on our mortgage. I hadn't been able to find a steady job with anything close to my former good salary, in years. Not months. Years. I know now that I wasn't the only person in America that was going through some very hard economic times. You hear about people losing their jobs, and homes, all the time. Being over 50 didn't help my chances, since any employer that would bring me on would have to pay more for my health care coverage and workers compensation premiums than they would for a job candidate in their 20's 30's , or 40's.

I was getting desperate because I just got a sense that no one was really going to give me a good look, or position, the older I got, and the longer I continued to be without a real 40 to 50 hour a week job. I started to contemplate about where I, and my family would go, where we would live, and what we would do to survive. I had missed two months of mortgage payments and had already received notice that if I didn't bring my account up to date by April 10th, 2009, that we would be considered to have defaulted on our loan, and foreclosure actions would be subsequently taken. My credit cards were also maxed out, since I had borrowed against them just to keep paying the bills. I had no job, no prospects for a good paying job, and bills up to my eyeballs. My choice, as I saw it, was either to just curl up in a fetal position, suck my thumb, and wait to financially die, or to go 100 % into trading stocks, and truly put my money, and my trading ideas, on the line. I could either give up, or come out fighting. What more did I have to lose? I had already lost almost everything. Doing nothing really wasn't an option, and I sure couldn't wait for some benevolent company, with financial problems of their own, to give me a job. So I decided to make trading and investing my job. In 2008, when most of the market was doing terribly, due to the high prices of gas at the pump, and various huge companies and banks failing, the majority of my trades ended up with me making a profit. I didn't even attempt to trade daily, at the time, but the majority of the few trades I did make that year had been successful. In most cases I had gone short.

That's when I thought about Stock Market Baseball. With default letters on the dining room table, with loan modification having been declined by the bank, and with foreclosure just around the corner I couldn't afford to take a long range approach to the investments and money that I still had in my stock market account. I needed to make money NOW! I needed to figure out a way to generate a few percent a day from trading stocks. If I could do that I could catch up on my late mortgage payments, pay down some bills, take care of my family, and keep the home that I, my wife, our three sons, and dogs and cats have called home for 18 years. I understand when folks feel like they don't have enough money to trade the markets with. I understand that that's the way they FEEL, but I also understand that even with a limited amount of money to invest and trade with, that you can make a living from trading stocks by focusing on making 1%, 2%, or 3% a day on your investment. Sometimes more. A lot more, like my experience with HGSI has shown. I've done it. I'm doing it. And so can you.

In my case, in 2009, a lot of my trading was done with $25,000 to $30,000. I sold long term investments from previous years at a loss just to be able to catch up on the mortgage, and then proceeded to put my trading ideas into action. My goal was to make at least $6,000.00 a month. That amount would be more than enough to pay the bills. I was already exceeding that goal by the end of April by making more than $8,000 on my trades that month. In previous years I had always been able to find stocks that were about to make a move, but my problem, based on buying into a long term buy and hold strategy, was that I held onto investments too long, even when they were losing money. I would initially invest in a stock, see the share price rise 5%, 10% or 20%, within a week, or so, and then fall in love with the stock, despite inevitable pullbacks in share price that sometimes completely wiped out my initial gain. But I just had to buy and hold.

Tough times can bring with them an ability to see things more clearly. I realized that while I had a good knack for finding good prospects to go long, or short, a stock for day or swing trades, that I negated that talent by being too passive and just buying and holding, despite what my eyes were telling me when I looked at the declining share prices that had wiped out my gains. I also realized that one of the reasons that I had bought into the buy and hold mentality was due to the difference in long term and short term capital gains tax rates. Trying to be prudent, and wanting to maximize my return on investment, I wanted to hold my investment for at least a year, and a day, so that the amount I had to pay the federal government on my long term gain would be almost half of what the short term capital gains tax rate would have me pay. That buy and hold strategy definitely had not been working for me lately. I still use that approach for stocks that I seem to understand well, and whose prospects truly are dynamic, long term. But for making money of a daily basis my focus and attention needed to be on short term moves, not long term. As for paying short term capital gains tax rates on short term trades and investments, if I have to pay those rates it's because I'm making money. I might mind paying more for short term capital gains, but it's the price I pay to have the opportunity to make money in this great country of ours.

It's amazing how, when your back is against the wall, when it seems like all hope is gone, that if you decide to not give up, and to focus on what's really important, and disregard the rest, how much clarity you start to see things with. As far as assessing the prospects for a trade, I no longer cared much about what a company did, what sector they were in, who their managers were, or any story touted, or shouted down, about a stock. I really only cared about what the technical indicators were telling me. I had definitely changed my investment philosophy from long term buy and hold to a "I need the money to pay the bills right now!" mode. And it was paying off quickly. On just 1%, 2%, or 3% a day.

  I wasn't born into a rich family. I didn't have hundreds of thousands, or millions, of dollars to trade with. But I can make, with the money that I do have to trade with, a good living for myself and my family. I think that you can too.

Focus on technical indicators

I like trading on technical indicators because the chart doesn't lie. If the volume indicator shows me that the amount of shares traded this month is twice the average of shares traded in the stock the previous month, and the share price hasn't changed too much, I'm going to interpret that information to mean that some deep pockets investors, or funds, are still accumulating shares, but don't want to cause the share price to rise too quickly, as it would if the large investor bought all of their intended investment with one huge buy.

The 12 day moving average crossing the 26 day moving average, or the 50 day moving average crossing the 200 day moving average also tells me something about the stock that I don't have to wait for some press release to tell me. Those moving average crossings tell me that a shorter term share price average is breaking through a longer term area of resistance, and that's important for me to know since that may indicate a continuing rise in the price per share, since longer term resistance is now support, and the share price might have 5%, 10%, 20% higher to go before running into overhead resistance again.

Another reason to learn how to use technical analysis and technical indicators is that, basically, people lie. Sometimes companies lie, as ENRON, WORLDCOMM, and other corporate examples have shown time, and time again. Someone can claim that their company has just discovered an invention that's better than sliced bread and that everybody will be buying it soon, but if the technical indicators don't tell me that the stock is going somewhere higher, or lower, in share price, than I really don't care too much about the verbal story being told.

Charts don't lie. Charts are just graphical representations of mathematical occurrences pertaining to the share price. They show me how many shares have been traded. They show me if the stock is currently overbought, or oversold, based on technical parameters being used. They show me where the next levels of support and resistance are. I don't have to guess, on a pullback, where the market maker might be pulling the share price down to. That's important information to trade on, or to assess, so that you don't sell prematurely on a momentary test of support, or resistance.

If I'm going to invest in a stock, long term, than I want to know everything about the stock that I can. I want to know all about what it does, and it's fundamental strengths, and weaknesses, but if I just want to find stocks that can make me 1 to 3% a day, or more, then I'm going to keep my focus and attention on the technical indicators.

Scouting the Prospects

Professional baseball scouts scour the country looking for players that show potential and talent to play in the big leagues. They review their stats and batting averages. They clock their pitches. They attend big games to see how the baseball prospects operate under pressure, and in the clutch. The objective is to find players that can be developed into everyday players that can play the infield, run down fly balls, hit for average, hit for power, and pitch with power, control, and speed to win ball games. Since the scouts can't be in all places, at all times, to find these prospects, they use regional scouting services that have compiled stats and game film on the players, in action. Based on what the scout sees on the stat sheet, and on the game film they then pursue the prospects they're interested in with more fervor and conviction, getting personally involved as they prepare to recommend investment in the player, for the minor, or the major, leagues.

It's not so different in Stock Market Baseball. But in this case, you are the Manager of the team, and it's primary scout. How do you find the stocks that you want to have running the bases for you? How do you find the stocks that you believe can score for you? Thankfully, the sources of information that you can use to find the right stocks to trade, and invest in, are easy to find just by using the internet.

There are so many technical indicators and tools to use, and refer to, to find good stocks to invest in. You can make your assessment of an investment, and trade, based on just a few indicators, as I like to do, or many, many more. Since there are only so many hours in the day, and over 16500 equities to choose from, not to mention bonds ETFs, and various commodities, I like to try to keep my analysis to those tools that make my analysis short, and sweet. Thankfully, there are quite a few online sites that encapsulate many technical indicators, all on the same page. The benefit of this is that you can make a visual analysis of several technical indicators, like support and resistance levels, volume increases, share price appreciation, or decline, and crossing moving average signals, as well as other indicators, all on one page. That saves you a lot of time and work. Like the old saying goes, "a picture is worth a thousand words" In the case of getting a visual handle on what a stock is doing, the information that these sites, and their charts provide, is invaluable. And most of the time the information on their sites is free. I'm going to discuss a few of these sites in the following pages.

Many of the big name investment information sites, like MSNBC.com [viii], Marketwatch.com [ix], and Yahoo.com [x] each have screening tools to help you find stocks meeting your trading parameters. I use them from time to time, especially Yahoo Finance [xi], for its' key statistics page, interactive chart, and message boards. But when I really want a one page visual graphical snapshot of a stock that I'm interested in I like to visit StockTA.com [xii], StockConsultant.com [xiii], StockChart.com, [xiv] and thinkorswim®.coms' ProphetCharts® [xv].

StockTA.com [xvi] has a great, simple to understand, one page chart covering the last 6 months. On the left hand side of the chart is a list showing levels of support and resistance, and how many times the share price has actually tested those levels. That's important information to know, since you get a better understanding about the strength of those levels of support and resistance, and how likely those levels could be to be taken out on any show of strength and momentum in the share price. StockTA.com also shows the percentage gain, or loss, for the day, in the share price, the percentage increase, or decrease, in the average daily volume, and a candlestick formation indicating whether what the candlestick is showing is bullish, or bearish for the stock price. There's more to StockTA.com, than just the simple to understand information contained on that one page, but for a simple mind like mine, it's truly very easy to use, and understand.

Before I came across StockTA.com, one of my favorite sites to go to for comprehensive chart information was StockConsultant.com[xvii]. Besides the outstanding chart information supplied, there are additional pages explaining candlestick formations, and point and figure charting. As you get deeper into charts and technical analysis, the more you'll appreciate all the tools that StockConsultant.com has to show you, and hopefully, learn to profit from that visual, graphical information. I still use StockConsultant.com to fill out my understanding of what's going on with a stock, and to take advantage of it's candlestick formations, as well as educating me on point and figure charting.

    A new site that has recently come to my attention is FinViz.com [xviii]. The information contained on this site on each stock is so comprehensive that it's going to take me a little time to get my mind around all that it has to offer. For numerical stats, in 72 different categories, as well as the graphical chart, I can't think of too many sites that offer you more, on one page, to review. Not only that, but Finviz.com also includes all recent press releases, and analyst coverage information, again, on the same page. I think that with time that I may be using this site quite a bit more.

    Here are a few sites offering some nice tools to use. One site, American Bulls.com [xix], provides a snapshot of candlestick chart formations and what they're suggesting for the share price direction. Candlestick charting has been used by Asian cultures for centuries to determine moves in prices for several hundred years. It would be a wise decision for any trader that wants to improve their game to get acquainted with candlestick charting. A picture paints a thousand words, and some of these candlestick charts do about the same thing. I wouldn't base all my trading on candlesticks, but I do think that they provide a nice visual tool to refer to, and review. StockConsultants.com [xx] also does a real nice job with it's candlestick charting lessons. Same thing with their P&F, Point and Figure, chart lessons. Take advantage of the information that these websites share.

One visual tool that's recently come to my attention is a Pivot Point calculator. xxi All you do is type in your stock symbol, and the calculator provides you with various points of support and resistance for the share price, based on the closing price for the shares the day before. That information is helpful in determining where good points to enter and exit a trade might be. There are many sites that offer these pivot point calculators. Find the one that works for you. StockTA.com already supplies this information on the left side of it's chart page, but it's always good to explore more sources of information

For the most part, during my day to day market monitoring activities, I use TDAmeritrade, Inc., and thinkorswim®. I understood the Command Center chart at TDAmeritrade, Inc., (now discontinued) and love all the technical tools immediately available to use with thinkorswim®s' ProphetCharts®. For me, that's all I need to monitor charts with, and trade with. Find what you're comfortable with, and use that.

What you don't want to do is fly blind, and trade on rumor. You don't just want to trade on an uniformed, unsupported hunch. Use the tools that other traders use to help them increase their odds of making a successful trade, and minimize their risk, at the same time. Knowledge is power. Knowing where to go to for information, and technical trading indicators, can mean money in the bank for you.

Get in the game

©2013 John George Campbell   stockmarketbaseball.com

Get in the game, Rookie.

To the experienced trader and investor, most everything that I'm going to cover in this chapter is pretty simple stuff. But for someone that's never traded, or invested before, it good to know some of the basics before you get started.

Before you start to play Stock Market Baseball with real money I think it would be smart to trade in a virtual trading platform. Not actual, real world, trades. Not with real money. There are a few sites that let you do this. Most online brokerage companies, like TDAmeritrade, Inc., Etrade, and Charles Schwab, as well as others, provide the new prospective investor and trader the opportunity to trade using a virtual trading platform, with virtual money, not actual money, to trade with. This way you can test your theories, and personal trading and investing skills out, before actually trading and investing with real money in the real stock exchanges.

    Since I use TDAmeritrade, Inc. as my online broker I also have access to their feature rich thinkorswim® trading platform. There's so much that this site offers that it would be best for you to try to try to access one of their virtual trading accounts to get acquainted with all the features thinkorswim® has to offer. They also provide daily market discussions, wrap-ups, and training sessions. I use their Fibonacci tool, superimposed over their ProphetCharts® tool, to visually see areas of support and resistance, as well as tools for drawing trading channels, trend lines, RSI overbought and oversold levels, etc.... Their screening tools, that help you find good prospects to trade and invest in, are also excellent. Their Sizzle Index is a great tool to access in order to find stocks experiencing dynamic moves and activity. Even though I don't trade options, at this moment, thinkorswim®s' option trading seminars, that I have attended, have also been really very good.

    Another virtual trading platform is the Virtual Stock Exchange Game found at MarketWatch.com [xxii]. Many people use this site, and you can actually play virtual stock exchange games with others that share similar interests, trading styles, and goals. All, with no real money at risk.

After you've tried your skills out at one of these various virtual trading sites, and are ready to actually trade, open up a brokerage account with one of the online brokers. I use TDAmeritrade, Inc., but there are many others that offer similar services. If you are going to start off with a trading account of less than $25,000.00, just be aware that you won't be able to make more than 3 round trip trades in a 5 day period of time without your account being flagged for pattern day trading. A round trip trade consists both the buying and selling of shares in the same investment, in the same day. Exceeding this 3 day limit in round trip trades within a 5 day period of time can be a problem for a couple of reasons. If you have been determined to have pattern day traded your trading account could be frozen for up to 90 days, your pattern day trading activity will be reported as such to the IRS, and you could be stuck not being able to get out of a trade, because your account has been frozen, maybe at just the time the share price is tanking, and you really need to be able to place a sell order. Does that scare you? It should. So, if you have a trading account with less than $25,000.00 liquid cash on hand to trade with, don't get into the habit of pattern day trading, and you won't have a problem.

Maybe, at first, as you're just dipping your toe in the waters, just trade 3 days a week, preferably, not in a row. Or, enter a trade on one day, hold the shares overnight, and then exit the trade the next day. In that situation, the pattern day trading rule doesn't apply. Or, Swing trade, rather than day trade. You'll trade less frequently, probably experience less daily stress, pay fewer fees and commissions, and likely be able to maximize a greater return on moves in the direction of the share price.

For those that can start trading with more than $25,000.00 it would probably be a good idea to actually fund your trading account with at least $30,000.00 to $35,000.00 Why? Because you will lose money on trades, from time to time, and the $35,000.00 will provide a good cushion above the $25,000.00 pattern day trading benchmark. Trading accounts with $25,000.00 or more in cash also qualify with many brokerage companies for trading using margin. What this means is that even though you may have $30,000.00 in cash in your trading account, that your trading leverage might actually be $90,000.00. Might be less, might be more, but being able to trade on margin can help you to maximize gains, since you can leverage your $30,000.00 to trade with up to $90,000.00, in my example. But just as it can maximize gains, it can also maximize losses, and wipe you out quickly. So use margin wisely. I've used it before to increase my monetary gains, and haven't had a margin call yet that I had to answer, but just be careful. The way you play the game, and get better at playing the game of Stock Market Baseball game, is to stay in the game. You can't win when you've been forced to the sidelines. So use margin accounts carefully. Because that leverage that the margin account affords you doesn't come free. You'll have to pay a fee, or interest, or both for the margin amount borrowed, because that's what you're doing. You're borrowing funds above the amount of cash that you actually have in your trading account to trade with. If managed correctly, this leverage can be very helpful in increasing your returns.

Now that you have your trading account funded, and are ready to trade, do this one thing every first hour of every trading day. Don't trade. Don't buy. Don't sell. Just Observe. The first hour of the trading day is considered by professional traders to be for rookies. And they will take advantage of you and your irrational exuberance to make a trade. So wait till the initial action of the first hour of the trading day is over, and a new trend is establishing itself, and then make your move. It may not be as exciting, but it will be a lot safer for you to try to develop the habit of waiting for the dust to settle before making your decision as to where, and when, you enter your trade.

Try to think logically, and without emotion, when you make your trade. Try to remove your emotions from the whole equation. You'll make better decisions, and execute better trades. I'm not telling you that you won't feel fear, elation, trepidation, uncertainty, joy, anger and a host of many other feelings when your trades are going good, or bad, because you will. But if you can control your emotions and impulses, you'll be a better trader and investor.

Use limit trades.

Now that the first hour of the trading day is over, and you're about to enter a trade, what should you do? For the most part, I like to use limit trades when I'm placing an order. What the limit order is telling the market maker is that I want to buy a certain amount of shares at a certain price, but if that price can't be delivered, than I don't want to pay more for shares than the limit price that I designated in my order. I will be happy to pay less, however, and sometimes, even though you've placed a limit order for 1000 shares of xyz company at $10.00 a share, there might be a few sellers that were selling for $9.98 right when you placed your order, and their sell order at $9.98 got swept up into your buy order, and you ended up getting some of the shares in your limit order for less than your limit price. That's always nice when that happens.

Don't use market orders.

    I know that there are some very experienced traders who would disagree with me on not using market orders, but I avoid using market orders, because if you enter a market order on a very volatile stock, where the volume is increasing rapidly, and price is either dropping, or spiking, you may end up buying, or selling your shares, with a market order far above, or far below, what you intended. Huh? It's like this. Say you've entered a market order to sell 10,000 shares of XYZ for $12.00, but terrible news regarding XYZ company gets released while your market order is in the cue. At the time you placed the order, the share price was $12.05, but within a few seconds after the terrible story came out the share price had plummeted to $6.00 a share, and that's where your market order to sell got executed. Ouch! What happened is that the market price for the shares had plunged to $6.00 just as your shares hit the market. Since you had a market order in place, and the new market price for XYZ was now $6.00, that's the price that your order got executed, or filled, at. So, in order to get the price that you want, or better, buying, or selling, it's safer, in my opinion, to use limit orders.

Use GTC, Good Till Canceled orders.

What if you're going out for the day, and want to enter a trade, but have a full day of business meetings scheduled.? You still want to place an order to buy, or sell, at a certain price, but won't be around to actually enter the order at the time your target price is arrived at . How can you get the trade you want executed at the price you want if you aren't going to be around to pull the trigger on the trade? Very simple. You can use a GTC order. Good till canceled. You can use this kind of order for a day, or for several months. You can include pre-market, and after-hours, or extended market time periods, with your good till canceled order. This way you can enjoy your day, and attend to other business, knowing that if, and when, your target price gets hit, that your order will get filled.

Sell Short, if you can't go long

If you decide that the company that you're tracking share's price is going to retreat, and you want to short that stock, you would enter an order to Sell Short. When the share price reaches your target price, lower than price you sold short at, you would then Buy to Cover the shares you borrowed to short with. You don't have to verbally talk to the broker in order to borrow shares to short. Online, it's all automated for you. If there are shares available to short, the broker will loan you the amount of shares that you want to borrow. If shares aren't available to short, then they won't.

As you can see, there are several ways to place orders. All the brokerage houses, whether online, or in your neighborhood, have professionally trained staff that can help you with your orders if you can't figure things out when you first begin. We all start somewhere.

Always double check your order entry for price, and amount of shares to be traded.

Remember this. It's a small detail, that can become a big problem if you don't pay attention to it. Whenever you enter an order to buy, or sell, using whatever order conditions that you want, always, ALWAYS, double check your order entry. The order for 10,000 shares of EXY that you want to buy for $10.00 a share is going to cause a much bigger dent in your trading account and a likely margin call from your broker if you failed to double check your order to see that you actually placed an order for 100,000 shares of EXY at $100.00 a share. Mistakes happen. Do your best to pay attention to eliminate mistakes. It's your money that you could be losing due to a small mistake.

You can't win them all

Every year, all around the country, and in parts of the world where the game of baseball is played, amateur baseball players drafts are held where kids in high school and college are discovered and drafted to play at various levels of the game for professional Baseball teams. Some kids that barely get drafted are sent to A, and AA minor league farm teams in order to work on their skills and understanding of the game. Others prospects, with considerable talent that put them right on the verge of getting called up to the major leagues might go to AAA level clubs. A few, maybe less than handful of players in the annual baseball draft go directly to the major leagues. When I was growing up there was one such player in the San Fernando Valley that had this kind of skill and baseball IQ. His name. Robin Yount. Robin Yount was drafted out of Taft High School in Woodland Hills in 1973 and started for the Milwaukee Brewers in his rookie season when he was just the age of 18. After 20 years in the big Leagues, Yount was voted into the Baseball Hall of Fame in Cooperstown, New York on the first ballot he was eligible for induction.

When major league scouts identify prospects to play ball at the professional level they dream of finding players like Robin Yount, but the truth of the matter is that many that get drafted never get beyond A and AA ball. They may have shown some promise, but somewhere along the line that promise, or potential, to make the big leagues doesn't pay off, for themselves, or the major league team that drafted them. Eventually they get cut. Or, they give up.

In Stock Market Baseball many of the stock prospects that we discover in the market also fail to pay off in a way that we had projected that they would, or could, if all the pieces fell into place. But for some reason they don't. And we're left wondering about "what if?" What If they got that big contract. What if they got that big important client. What if they could have struck oil instead of dry well after dry well. What if the government would just authorize the new energy saving and producing technology so that more investors would invest in the company and the technology? What if the drug that the company spent millions and millions of dollars for in research and development costs hadn't failed during phase III trials. What if ? What if ? What if ?

You might be able to sense that I've experienced a few moments of "What if?" during my experience trading and investing in the stock market, and you would be correct. Anybody that's ever traded the stock market for any period of time has experienced losses. While I'm not familiar with all of Warren Buffet's trades, I can guarantee that somewhere along the way that this legendary investor has also experienced losing money on some of his investments. It happens. To everyone. No one is immune to this occurrence. But you can learn to manage your risk in order to minimize your losses when they do occur.

Use Stop Losses.

Use actual stop losses, or mental stop losses. If you have a life outside of trading, where you go to an office, plant, store, hospital, business or other location to spend your working hours on something other than trading, than it might be wise for you to set stop losses 8% to 10% below your new found gains, or even below your original entry price for the shares. Why should you do this? Well, if you are away from tracking the markets, and all of a sudden a devastating piece of news pertaining to your stock is released, it's very possible that the share price could plunge 50%, or more in a few minutes, or hours. By the time you get home, if you haven't used a stop loss to protect your downside, you will be rudely surprised with a dramatically lower stock price than what you had seen the share price trading at before you left for work. If your investment in that stock had been substantial, you would also see a substantial loss in the value of your portfolio. So instead of risking losing a great percentage of the value of your shares and portfolio, by setting a stop loss at 8% to 10% below your most recent high, you can limit your loss to that 8% or 10%, whatever the case may be. 8% might be a hit in the wallet, but no where near as bad as what a 50% to 70% hit would cost you.

Use mental stops

If you are actively trading, then you might want to choose mental stops, instead of actual stop losses. Why? Because since you are actively tracking your trades and investments, you are in a better position to act swiftly to sell shares on the immediate release of bad news. In most cases it will take a few minutes for the impact of the news to be full understood by the market. During that time period you will have an opportunity to sell, at maybe less than a 5% pullback from the recent high. But you have to act swiftly. Once the bad news is understood by the market place, the fall in share price can be swift and devastating. This does not mean that I don't think that active traders should not use actual stop loss orders. It's just that, if you are actively trading you will be in a much better position to act swiftly on negative news.

On the other hand, a plus for using mental stops with stocks that are showing some price volatility while they are on the cusp of releasing an important report is that market makers may use this heightened volatility to take out all actual stops in order to force the sale of shares by traders and investor using actual stop loss orders. Why would they do that? Because market makers are traders too. Like it or not, they can sense, and many times know, what's happening with the stock behind the scenes minutes, or even seconds, before you could ever know. And with that slim margin of advantage it's in their best interest to force the sale of shares by those using stop losses, so that they, the market maker, can replenish their inventory of shares before good news is released that takes the share prices higher. Some hedge fund managers, utilizing very powerful algorithmic trading systems, play this game too. And here's another piece of information that you may not like. Insider trading still goes on. Every market day. Some insiders, hedge funds, or behind the scenes investors, may be using the market maker to manipulate the share price in order to persuade you to sell, so that they can buy those shares for themselves.

" But, that's not fair !"

Fair, or not, insider trading still occurs in the market, and sometimes insiders, knowing that a game changing event is going to happen for the company, also use the market makers to place trades that manipulate the share price lower, in order take out stop losses that have been set before recent share price highs. This kind of market action is referred to in several ways, like "shaking the tree for low hanging fruit", "Shaking out the weak hands" and other variations on that theme. In other words, the game, in that instance, is to motivate some weak willed, nervous, emotionally drained and scared shareholders to sell, so that others can acquire more shares. Simple as that.

A more experienced trader and investor can recognize this kind of activity, and decide to either sell at their mental stop, or refuse to fall for the ploy at all, and hold on to their shares beyond the 8% to 10% momentary pullback, sensing, and knowing, from the depth of their own due diligence, and prior experience with similar situations, that the company is on the verge of something big, and aren't going to be shaken out of their shares. For experienced traders, it's a judgment call. Handle it in the way that best suits you. Newer traders might want to use actual stop losses until you've arrived at a good understanding, through experience, about how the stop loss game can be played by the market maker, and others, that want your shares prior to important game changing events for a company. Use similar methods with your short positions too. Just place your short trade stops above where you entered your short position, or above where the share price has dropped to since you went short, in order to protect your gains.

Choose your entry and exit targets carefully.

Something else to consider is where you enter and exit a trade. My suggestion to you is to get very familiar with support and resistance pivot points, or retracement levels. Why? Because these levels tell you graphically, and visually, where the share price might drop to, to test support below the current price level, or resistance above the current share price.

How does this apply to risk management and loss control with regards to the share price? Let's say that the current share price is $9.60, and from your review of support and resistance levels, Fibonacci levels, for example, that support for the share price is about 1% lower at $9.50, but the next resistance level above is at $10.00. This could mean, on a day when the share price is trending higher, that your current downside risk, before you reach support is just 1%, but your upside reward spread is 4% higher. The risk reward ratio in this situation would appear to be 1:4, with the upside move looking to be a better likelihood to provide a nice gain. If the opposite 4:1 factor presented itself, where you're just 1% from overhead resistance, and 4% from a lower support level, then I might short that scenario, if the share price bounces off upside resistance, and heads back lower. If it breaks above resistance, than you might be seeing a new higher trading range beginning to be established, and need to wait until the range is established, or not. If it doesn't form, and the share price drops back down through the recent resistance level, you could still make money with a short trade until the share price reaches lower support.

Diversify.

Another way to minimize your risk of loss is to diversify your assets. In other words, don't put all your eggs in one basket. Spread the risk. Not just to other stocks, but to other stocks in other sectors. At the same time, don't invest in more stocks than you can reasonably manage and trade. Maybe a handful, or less. If one stock declines in share price, it's very possible that another stock, in another sector, might be moving higher. Here's a caveat to the spread the risk wisdom. If you are fortunate to find a big winner that's just won a major contract, or has experienced a very positive, game changing event for the company, you might want to listen to what Andrew Carnegie, the famous 20th century industrialist and philanthropist had to say about diversification, in that event. "Put all you eggs in a basket...And WATCH THAT BASKET !"

I guess I practice a bit of both ends of the spectrum regarding this method of using diversification to manage and minimize risk. Frankly, I think Andrew Carnegie did too. On a second read of his famous quote he mentions all of his eggs in a basket, not just a singular egg. So he was watching several eggs in his basket. Not just one. Your basket is your portfolio. Your eggs are the companies, whose shares that you trade. Your bigger basket could include other items like annuities, bonds, commodities, and real estate, as well as permanent life insurance. Unless it is of a permanent kind, life insurance policies won't grow interest in a tax deferred manner. But as a foundation from which to pursue you other investments, life insurance, even term life insurance, needs to be in most traders, and investors, financial basket. Health insurance too, since a catastrophic health care crisis can wipe you out, as it had me, making it almost impossible to remain trading the market since trading accounts may need to be sold off in order to pay for medical bills. Don't think it can't happen to you. It can.

Use Calls and Puts.

Another way of hedging your trades is to use call or put options. Since I don't presently use options I'm not going to get into great detail about how to use them to manage risk, except to suggest taking a seminar presented by a company like thinkorswim.com or other companies like them, who focus a lot of attention on how to use option strategies. Traders and investors alike use options as part of their overall strategies. For the time being, I don't. While I do see value in using options, I don't like the finite aspect to using options. Options carry with them expiration dates. Because of the finite nature of the option contract I'm hesitant to use them right now. Until I grow more sophisticated, and develop a better understanding of how best to use them, and under what circumstances, I'll leave option trading, and usage, to others.

Many traders make money trading option contracts. It's not in my comfort zone yet, and one of the primary purposes of writing this book is to share with you what I know, through experience, that's helped me make money, and successful trades in seemingly very tough market conditions of 2009 and 2010. I made more than 550% in my portfolio in 2009 , and 200% return on investments in 2010. What I understand about trading and investing is helping me to beat most of the biggest fund managers and traders in the markets. That's what my experience has taught me about trading. When Options become more a part of my strategy, and I am more experienced with using them in a way that I believe can help my readers, I will share with others how I use them successfully.

"Cut your losses and let your winners run".

This is a common saying in trading and investment circles. Eventually, if you're holding onto to losing stocks, whose immediate future doesn't look like it going to get much better very soon, then cut your losses, and use the remaining money to regroup and find better trades to make gains with. Remember this saying when you're rationalizing why you're holding onto a stock, whose share price has dropped more than 20%. It's tough on the mind to take your losses, but holding onto them, most of the time, does you no good. At the very least, when tax loss selling season comes around at the end of the year, cut your losses then, and write off those losses against your gains when you file your taxes.

Have an accountant, preferably a Certified Public Accountant, help you with this. A good CPA is probably the single most important professional adviser that every trader should have.

A good rule of thumb that many traders and investors use to minimize their losses is to set a 8% to 10% limit on how much they are willing to accept as a loss on their investment, before they cut their loss. That's a pretty good rule, but keep in mind that many volatile stocks can drop 20% on one day before fantastic news that propels the share price 50%, 100%, 200% and more, higher. I've seen that happen several times over the years. I guess my approach is to try to understand the nature of your investment once you've found them through technical analysis. Understand what the company does. Understand what kind of progress may be on the immediate horizon. Understand the games that can be played by traders with better access to insider information in order to take the share price down so that they can motivate others, like you, to sell before positive news comes out. Despite all the rules and regulations meant to put a stop to insider trading, don't kid yourself into thinking that insider trading doesn't happen. It happens all the time. Technical analysis can help to even out the playing field, despite what you might not know about what's going on behind the scenes of the stocks that you trade in.

A few years back I was swing trading ABP, Abraxas Petroleum. I was swing trading, sometimes for 2%, or 3% going long, and then immediately going short for another 2%, or 3%, when the market maker pulled the share price back, all in the same day. It was a fun stock to trade, since the market makers' moves seemed so obvious to me. During this time ABP was primarily an oil exploration company, with no discoveries, or producing wells, to speak of. While I was trading it, the share price was generally trading in the mid $2 dollar range. Soon, it started to move to the high 2's, and then, all of a sudden it started to drop in share price down to the $2.15 level for a better than 25% drop in share price, on not very significant volume. Basically, a low volume pullback. The low volume pullback told me that technically, few strong hands, or confident, knowledgeable investors, were selling into this pullback. The only ones selling were weak willed, psychologically exhausted investors, or traders, that didn't understand what ABP was about, or that hadn't done a bit of due diligence, at all, into ABP. It wasn't long before ABP started to move back into the higher $2 range again, and then, BOOM ! News was released that they had hit oil. All of a sudden the share priced broke above $3.00, for the first time, in a long time. The share price rallied over the next few months to $9.00. I didn't take the whole ride, as I sold in the mid 8 dollar range. But my point is, that if you have done your due diligence on your investment, than it might be wise to not automatically set an 8 to 10% stop below your current trading level, where you might get shaken out by the market makers that know what loss limits lots of traders use, and will test those levels in order to steal shares from you before big game changing news comes out that takes the share price much higher.

I've traded other stocks in the past, where a similar set up of a swift and deep decline in share price on low volume was seen before a several hundred percent rise in share price took place. But back in those days, I hadn't taken the time to really study technical indicators, or technical analysis. I was primarily using fundamental analysis to find these stocks, but was flying blind when it came to understanding support and resistance levels. Basically, I was benefiting from some very good dumb luck, but I really didn't know what I was doing, technically.

Once again, knowledge is power. Fundamental analysis will tell you about what a company does, how much money it makes and spends, how much money it's expected to make and spend, etc..., but technical analysis can provide technical signals to help you know when to buy, and when to sell, and when to hold through tests of the share price. If I had known about technical analysis back when I was trading these companies, I may have been able to make better decisions on when to buy and sell, and made more money from those trades. I did well, but I could have done better had I taken the time to educate myself about technical analysis, and technical buy and sell indicators.

Keep your head in the game.

©2013 John George Campbell stockmarketbaseball.com

Keep your head in the game

There are a lot of investors and traders that consider technical analysis, and technical indicators to be like reading tea leaves, or practicing some kind of voodoo trading magic. Some of these same investors and traders seem to think the best way to trade and invest is to go with the hot stock recommendation from some of the talking heads on the TV, or internet investment sites, without doing any due diligence themselves to understand what they're investing and trading in.

So much the better for me, or other traders and investors that do take the time to educate ourselves about the details , and not just trust the pontifications of the perceived "experts". By doing your own research you can put yourself at an advantage to these know nothings that trade the markets blindly, and at the very least, you can learn how to verify, and validate that information that you're getting from the investment experts makes sense, or not. Because, when it comes down to it, the final decision to invest, or trade, to buy, or sell, lies with you, the investor, or trader. No one else.

In previous chapters I've mentioned a few online sites that can help you to learn technical analysis. They being thinkorswim®, StockTA.com, StockConsultant.com, and TDAmeritrade, Inc. There are numerous other sites, some sponsored by online brokerages like Etrade, Charles Schwab, Marketwatch, and others. If monetary exchanges and commodities are what you're interested in trading, than FOREX.com [xxiii] would be a good place to seek out information.

There are also many books that you can refer to in order to get a better understanding of charting and technical analysis. One of the books that I've learned from is How Charts Can Help You In The Stock Market by William Jiler, OTC publications[xxiv]. There are many books on stock charts, but this one was one of the easiest for me to read and understand. I picked it up from a garage sale, as I do most of the books I've read. I also picked up a first edition of the famous book The Intelligent Investor, by Benjamin Graham[xxv], with the original dust jacket, for 10 cents, at the same garage sale. Another great book to read pertaining to market psychology and contrarian investing is Contrarian Investment Strategy by David Dremen[xxvi]. His discussions about mob psychology, and how it's wise to trade against the mob, or mob think, is very insightful.

The internet has a wealth of blogs and websites created by various investment professionals with lots of educational resources and intelligent discussions on their sites. Two of my favorites are SEEKING ALPHA [xxvii], and THE HARD RIGHT EDGE. Both sites are very different from one another. SEEKING ALPHA is very slick and professional in appearance. It includes contributions from a great deal of traders and technicians, with links to their sites, as well. THE HARD RIGHT EDGE, featuring the insights of Alan Farley [xxviii], doesn't appear to be as slick, but don't let the appearance fool you. Mr. Alan Farley, self titled THE MASTER SWING TRADER, provides a great deal of in depth explanation of chart and technical patterns, and indicators, that the person serious about learning technical analysis would do well to take the time to get acquainted with. He also includes commentary and links by other investing and trading professionals. Both of these sites are information rich, but the HARD RIGHT EDGE seems to me to be more specifically educationally oriented when it comes to teaching the reader about charting, technical analysis, swing trading, and buy and sell signals.

StockCharts.com is also very rich in information about technical indicators, candlestick formations, and point and figure charting. I highly recommend reviewing the free chart school link, where various technical indicators are very well explained.

These are just three of the many websites devoted to the discussion of trading stocks. Take the time to do some of your own research to find stock discussion blogs and websites that are helpful to you in learning how to trade. I think the time spent in independent research, and analysis, is time very well spent.

But the game is fixed. I can't compete.

Ha! Ha! I agree. The game is fixed. It's not supposed to be. It's supposed to be a free market. It's supposed to be fair .The S.E.C., the Securities and Exchange Commission[xxix], is supposed to be policing the trading of equities, and securities, and you do read about them making a bust from time to time, of some deep pockets hedge fund, or investment bank, or some boiler room penny stock operation. But insider trading still exists. Dark pool security transactions, where big institutional sellers, and buyers, are paired with other institutional sellers and buyers, outside of regular market avenues, moving massive amounts of shares without affecting the share price a penny, still happen. Market makers getting hints of impending news before you know, trade on that advanced knowledge. Yes. They do. Every day of every trading week. The playing field isn't level. The game isn't fair. It's definitely slanted toward the big dogs. But you can still make money if you know what the technical indicators are telling you.

That's one of the reasons why the internet, and data information provided by some very creative, and intelligent financial software designers, can help to level the playing field. If you aren't accessing the great amount of free technical and fundamental investment analysis sites on the internet, you have no one to blame about being in the dark about your trades, but yourself.

I review charts of various stocks every day, most of the time during the market hours, and then after the market hours, and then again, after supper. I don't spend a lot of time on stocks whose charts don't immediately speak to me. If I can't see a chart pattern looking like it's ready to break higher, or lower, than I move on to the next chart. So many stocks. So little time. Here are some of the stock information sites that have worked for me in the past when trying to find stocks whose charts are indicating a nice move, one way, or the other.

StockTA.com I found this site via a Google search for technical analysis sites for stock trading. For a guy like me, with limited technical analysis training, I found that I could review support and resistance levels, basic candlestick chart indicators, and basic technical indicators like MACD, Stochastics, RSI, and volume indicators, all on one page. Prior to this I had been using StockConsultant.com for their thorough chart analysis, but I didn't like Stockconsultant's automated read of what the chart patterns were indicating. While their opinions seem to be based on artificial intelligence, and algorithms, I found myself doing better with my trades when I trusted my own reads, rather than what StockConsultant.com was telling me.

As for StockTA.com, for me, the basic, straightforward graphical information provided in their one page chart, with support and resistance levels printed on the left hand side of the chart, was more than enough to give me a good handle on what the stock was about, price direction wise. For me, the "KISS, Keep It Simple, Stupid" adage came to mind, as it applied to what my feeble mind could understand and use to make better trading decisions. StockTA.com, gave me the highly graphical informative information that I needed.

Yahoo Finance. I'm sure that Microsoft and Google also have their financial site. In fact, I know that they do. But I've been participating on the Yahoo Finance page message board for years, so I have an understanding of how they work, and I get involved with the message board sites of the stocks that I'm investing in. Some of the posters are very well informed, and industry savvy. Way beyond my level of knowledge. But you also have to understand how to gauge honest information from misdirection. I don't know how you do that except by life experiences, where you learned how to differentiate truth from fiction. Some people are better at this than others. That's where your internal ability to make wise judgments for yourself comes in. Because, with trading, when it comes right down to it, you are the one that's responsible for your trades. Not the guy that recommended the trade to you. Not the guy that advised you not to trade that stock. But you. The buck stops with you. You make the decisions, based on your judgment of the information that you've received and analyzed. The way I play this game, no one else is accountable for what I do. It's all on me. Can you deal with that? Can you accept responsibility for your own investment decisions? Or are you the type that blames other persons for your bad decisions? Only you can answer that question.

Yahoo Finance provides a great deal of market information, and individual stock information. When I've identified a stock that I want to know more about I access the Yahoo key statistics page for that stock to find out how large the float is and what the short ratio is, as well as how many shares trade, on average, per day, and if that volume has increased over the last 10 days, or last few months. I then access the home site of the company whose stock I'm investigating, and read about what they're all about, what they make, what their main products are, what their management team is like, and then who some of the major institutional investors, and insiders are. I will then visit the message board to find out if there's any signs of any intelligent life form there, in order to pick their brains for a street level understanding of what makes this stock tick. Prior to visiting the message board I will have already reviewed an interactive chart, with Bollinger bands, RSI, MACD, volume indicators, and moving average indicators, like the Golden Cross, showing on the chart. If all the pieces fit, then I'll consider trading the stock.

Game Day

When you read about the training habits, and in game practices, of great teams, and great athletes, you find that those that succeed beyond what others do, is because the great ones will do what the talented, but undedicated teams, and players, won't do. And sometimes, that extra effort isn't really extra, at all. It's just doing what you should be doing to practice, and prepare, and play in a manner that helps you to do your best every day. Training for, practicing for, and actually actively trading stocks, if that's what you decide to do to make money, requires no less focus and attention. You can make money from trading stocks, part time, but I think it's much more to your advantage if you give a full time attitude and focus to your trades and investments.

After you've practiced screening for stocks to trade; and learned about how to use technical analysis and technical indicators in order to buy and sell stocks, and after you've put in quite a few hours to do your due diligence on the stocks that you want to invest in, then you may be ready for game day.

Game Day in Stock Market Baseball, is every trading day of the week, month, and year. Just like I want to focus on hitting for 1%,2%, and 3% daily returns, let's focus on a singular trading day, and how I approach playing my game.

I'm on the west coast, so my hours of play will be three hours behind someone playing Stock Market Baseball in New York City, two hours behind someone playing in Chicago, and one hour behind someone playing in Denver. For someone playing in Japan, where baseball is a big national sport, I'll be getting up to get my day started just as the Asian markets are closing. So when I reference time, I'm referencing Pacific Standard Time hours.

4:30 AM, PST . (Pacific Standard Time)

I get up and go downstairs, with my three dogs, while the rest of the family is still sleeping. I make a 8 cup pot of coffee, half of which I'll drink, with the other half left for my sons, when they wake up. I turn on the TV to Bloomberg News$_{xxx}$, and then start up my laptop and log on to my TDAmeritrade, Inc. account, while in another browser window I log onto my thinkorswim® account, and bring up their ProphetCharts® for whatever stock I want to review at the time. After having my trading platforms up and running I then access Yahoo Finance in order to visit the message boards of the stocks that I am currently trading or have on my watch list. All of these activities are done before the pre-market opens at 5 :00AM, PST.

5:00 AM, PST to 6:30AM, PST.

The pre-market opens. There are many professional traders that don't trade the pre-market, at all. And, in general, neither do I. But I have been surprised on several occasions, by news released right at the beginning of the pre-market hours that causes the share price of a stock to spike higher, or lower, quite suddenly, and on healthy volume. So, as a form of risk management, I like to be up and monitoring the markets during the pre-market hours, just in case one of these surprising events occurs. The pre-market hours are also a great time to review what's happened in the Asian markets the night before. What happens in Japanese, Chinese, and Korean markets is important to get an understanding of since they are important players in science and technology, finance, automotive manufacturing, and other major industries and sectors. If the Asian markets are down in some sector, than it may follow that our own markets in that sector will also trend lower during our trading day.

Another benefit about being up and ready in the pre-market is the morning briefings that you can review on the internet, and through TV financial news sites like CNBC[xxxi], Bloomberg, or Fox Business News[xxxii]. I prefer Bloomberg, because their format seems to be more focused on news and market discussion, rather than on the personalities presenting the stories. I just want the news. Not the spin. Give me the news and I'll come to my own conclusions. So, as far as that's concerned, Bloomberg just works better for me.

6:30 AM, PST.

The Markets open. I rarely do any trading during the first hour of the day. I actually rarely do any day trading. But I want to have my TDAmeritrade, Inc. platform in full screen, so that I can monitor all of my watch list, and portfolio at one time, while also monitoring level II activity for a couple of stocks that I have more of my focus on for that day. Level II allows you to see the amount of bids and asks in the trading cue, and information pertaining to the volume size of those bids and asks. This is important to know, as a large bid may be providing a certain level of support at that time while a large volume ask might be acting as resistance. And level II will show that to you.

I also like to open up a couple of charts of stocks that I am particularly interested in keeping track of that day. With each of these charts I also include Volume, MACD, RSI, and Bollinger Band technical indicators. As for the line type used to graph the chart with, I like to use Japanese candlesticks. I can see candlestick formations like dojis, spinning tops, and hammers easier in the chart that way.

In another browser window, that I've have my thinkorswim® Prophetcharts® up in, I also superimpose a Fibonacci retrace-ment ladder from the bottom of a recent move to it's top. The ladder created will show levels of support and resistance for the stock's share price between the low and high prices used to create the Fibonacci ladder. These levels are important to know about when pullbacks start to occur, or when the share price starts to move higher. The levels of support and resistance give you specific targets to aim at, without having to guess about where a rally might stop, or a pullback might end.

While all of this is going on I'll check in and out of the Yahoo finance message board sites for stocks in my portfolio, or watch list, many times throughout the day. If there's an interesting discussion, I'll try to add my two cents. Sometimes there's just some of the regular investors just hanging around, sharing jokes, or slices of life on the message board. And that's good too, as lighthearted moments like that makes the days, weeks, and months of online trading go by a bit easier. But sometimes, if you've got some really very good message board participants on your message board, you can find posted links to news pertaining to your investments that the company hasn't even made public yet. Sometimes the company might think that the news found wasn't "material" for the investors to know about, but for the investors, every bit of information pertaining to their investment is important to know about, since it may be a sign of strength or weakness to assess, as far a personal risk management of your investments, is concerned. You can also learn a lot about trading, and other investments, from financial message board discussions, since all the participants, for the most part, are investors, or traders, and have opinions as to what kind of technical, or fundamental, tools work best for them. You don't know everything. You can't know everything. But if you can come away with learning something new that can help you to be a better trader or investor, than the time spent conversing with others on financial message boards, like those at Yahoo Finance, can prove beneficial.

7:30AM, PST.

After the flurry of first hour trading is over, and that trend is beginning to reverse itself, if I was a day trader, I might think about entering a trade now, but going in the opposite direction of the early trend. So if the first hour took the share price higher, I would look for a sign of weakness, and reversal in the chart, and go short. If the share price started the day with the share price falling, I would look for a sign of a reversal to the upside, and enter a long trade. I'm writing in generalities here, but that seems to be the way these moves are best played. But you can't make them in a vacuum. If all of the rest of your technical signals are saying to buy, then buy. If your technical indicators indicate selling, then sell. But eventually, the direction of the share price will reverse itself, since share prices are constantly moving up, and down.

If you want to day trade, but don't want to make a lot of trades in a day, in order to keep your fees and commissions to a minimum, you might want to do what many other traders do. Enter a trade early in the day, after the first trading hour is over, and then close your trade within the last hour of the trading day, probably within the last half hour.

Why? Because, at the end of the day, if you're trading a stock whose overall trend has been higher for the last several days, or weeks, then you might benefit from short covering going into the close, taking the share price higher by a few percentage points.

Again, I'm writing about this kind of trade, in generality. To execute this trade specifically, there's more to it than just buying earlier in the day, and closing the trade in the last hour. There's technical indicators to consider, like Bollinger Bands, MACD, and RSI, as well as the overall trend line of the stock in question. The more that you learn about how to use technical indicators, and technical analysis, especially when it comes to day trading, the better. And keep your eyes open for late day press releases regarding your investments, as well as level II bid and ask levels. All of this information can have a bearing on the success, or failure, of your trade.

9:00AM to 10:00AM, PST

I think of this time as sort of a quiet time in the trading day. Volume seems to slow down a bit. It's lunch time on the east coast, when many New York City traders take a break, and regroup a bit from the first hours of the trading day. It's also at about this time that investment firms research departments provide updates on what's happening with the markets, in general, and the company's investments, in particular. With that information the final three hours of the trading day are about to commence.

10:00 AM, PST to 1PM, PST.

The last three hours of the regular trading day. Many times the 10 o'clock hour will resemble the 9 through 10 o'clock hour, at first. But between 11:30 and 12:00 you may see volume beginning to rise again, as well as share price volatility. The volatility increases even more between 12.30 PM, PST, and 1:00 PM, PST, as day, momentum, and short term traders close their long, and short positions. This last hour of trading is when you too, should close a short term long, or short position, if it's reached your target price . It might also be wise for you to close all your shorter term positions by the close of trading on Friday, since a weekend is a long time to hold onto a position, without knowing what kind news that could effect the market might be released over the weekend. Do I do this? No. Not always. But I'm more of a longer term swing, or position trader, so I'm not focused on the shorter term window. But I know that many traders with a shorter term game plan do close their positions daily, and especially, weekly. Depending on what kind of trader you determine yourself to be, and under what circumstances, do what's best for you.

1:00 PM to 2:00 PM, PST.

Daily review time. First hour of the after hours, or extended, market period. During the first 15 minutes of this time period some of the last trades of the day get settled and get reflected in the share price. Sometimes, in the first hour of the after hour trading period, companies will also release news pertaining to important positive, or negative, company events. It's important to not turn your computer off during this first hour of the after hours, just in case these news events occur that could have a positive or negative effect on the share price of your investments. In general, terrible news is released in the after-hours on a Friday, and great, game changing news is released in the pre-market hours on Mondays, or another day early in the week. Why? Because the hope is that the negative effect of bad news, released in the after-hours trading period on Friday, will be dissipated over the weekend, and that positive effect of good news, released early in the week, can be maximized throughout the remainder of the week as momentum, day, and swing traders, pile on the stock, and the law of supply, and demand, takes the share price higher.

2:00 PM to 5:00PM, PST.

OK. For me, this is nap time, followed by exercise time, only if nothing significant has been announced in the first hour of the extended trading period. Nap time, because I need to catch up on the sleep I give up in order to wake up at 4:30, so that I can be ready for the pre-market. After an hours nap, I'll take a bike ride for an hour, or two, and then come back to shower, and then start to prepare for supper, if my wife isn't making one of her delicious meals.

So. That's my game day. Pretty much every day. But that's not the end of it, really. Because after supper, and after taking the dogs for a walk, around **7:00 PM, PST**, I'll start up the laptop again, and review the charts of the companies in my portfolio, watch list, and other stocks that showed great activity that day. With the television on a news channel, or sports event, in the background, I'll also check, and participate in, the message boards for some of the stocks that I have a positions in. By about 10:00PM, PST, after having reviewed the previous days activities, and several charts of current positions, and new investments to consider, I end my day, and go to bed, with my day time associates, my three dogs, joining me in getting some sleep before the next trading day begins.

Succeed because you have to.

©2013 John George Campbell   All Rights Reserved

Succeed because you "Have to"

Some great baseball players are born natural athletes. They've been blessed with speed, strength, great eye-hand coordination, great vision, great power, and as they play the game of baseball over the years, great baseball IQ, or great understanding of the game. Other great players weren't born great. Even the great natural athletes that became great baseball players weren't born great baseball players. They developed their skills and became great baseball players, over time. Some great baseball managers were adequate baseball players, but better managers, because they understood the nature of the game, game situations, and how to maximize the opportunities set before them.

One of my favorite baseball managers of all time is Tommy Lasorda, of the Los Angeles Dodgers. From what I've read about him, Tommy Lasorda wasn't a great pitcher. By most accounts, Tommy Lasorda wasn't even a great athlete. But when you look at the effect that he had on the Dodger players that played for him on the Dodger teams that he managed, and the results that he achieved in taking the Los Angeles Dodgers to National League, and World Series Championships, Tommy Lasorda proved himself to be one of the greatest Baseball managers of all time.

Why ? Because, over the years, Tommy Lasorda mastered the game of baseball. He learned how to get the most out of his players. He learned how to inspire his players to believe in themselves, their teammates, and in their abilities to get the job done to achieve the goals that they had to achieve, both personally, and as a team. They won because they had to win. The believed that they could win. So they won. Tommy Lasorda instilled that in them. He was one of the most light hearted and fun loving baseball coaches of all time too, but none of that got in his way of achieving the goals that he had to achieve because he believed he could. There might have been other managers that were better understanding statistics, though Lasorda knew statistics too. But there were few that understood, better than Lasorda, how to maximize the opportunities presented to him every day during the baseball season, and how to get his players to rise to a level that he knew that they could rise to.

It's not so different when you trade stocks for a living. Some guys, using algorithmic computer programs, actually spend less time than I do preparing for, and monitoring their investments, during the day. Some of them only focus on the first, and last hour, of the trading day. Some of these guys were blessed with natural intellectual abilities to understand mathematical and technical formulas and technical information. Compared to these guys, my more manual way of doing things must seem like "Old School", and maybe even a bit Cave Man, by comparison. But for me, my way works, partly because the few technical indicators that I do understand, I seem to understand how to use pretty well.

Being a liberal arts, creative sort of a guy, and singer by natural talent, I seem to have an artist's, outside-the-box, intuitive approach to understanding what I'm seeing, and sensing, when I'm reviewing technical indicators for a stock, and the intangible value, or lack of value, of the stories being spun around a stock. I think I got some of that sense of intuition from my mother, and from the negotiating skills, and styles, of guys I had worked for that were heavy on street smarts, and light on academic rigidity. What these guys hadn't learned in class, or from books, they more than made up for in how they were highly skilled in reading human nature, weaknesses, strengths, needs, and wants, and how to assess whether what they were hearing was true, or not, and whether the person that they were dealing with had the same ability to read those basic qualities of human nature. Now that I focus most of my trading around the statistical likelihood of certain things happening, due to a better understanding of how to use technical indicators, and analysis, it's the street smarts that I developed, and how to read human nature, that's helped me to assess fact, from fiction, when I'm assessing the validity of the spin around a stock when it doesn't coincide with what the technical indicators are telling me.

So, for the reader that thinks that they were never very good at math, or science, or anything technical, but that they have good reasoning skills, and a good ability to read human nature, don't convince yourself that trading stocks using technical analysis is not for you. When I was in high school and college I convinced myself that I was no good at math and science. It wasn't until many years later, when I had to pass series 6 and 63 exams to keep my job in the insurance business, and ended with the highest scores in the region for my company, that I started to think that maybe I was better at math and statistics than I had ever given myself credit for. I had studied and passed that exam, because I had to pass. I had no other choice. I had to. So, I passed. The reason I started to do really well trading stocks is because I learned technical analysis, and how to trade using this technical information. Why? Because my back was against the wall, and I absolutely had to.

So don't convince yourself you can't do a thing because you've never thought that you could do it before. That's called "stinkin' thinkin'". Don't think that way.

Make your perceived obstacle a goal that you must achieve. Not might achieve, but must achieve. You have to. If at first you don't succeed, try again. And again. And again. Until you achieve your goal. In my case, the times when I've made personal breakthroughs have come when I absolutely had to make breakthroughs. No ifs, ands, or buts, about it. I had to. I couldn't allow myself to accept a "might happen" mentality. I had to adopt a "must happen" mentality in order to achieve the results that I wanted, needed, and would be happy with.

There's a lot of psychic rewards that you gain when you achieve personal goals that you had previously thought were impossible for yourself to attain. Remove the impossible thought from your mindset. Stop limiting yourself. Work for, study for, and spiritually and psychically fight for, those goals that are important to you. Do not accept that you can't achieve the impossible. People achieve impossible things everyday. All I'm saying in regards to understanding technical analysis is that, if you're not a technical type, or a mathematician, or technically inclined, that technical analysis is not impossible to understand and master. Look at me. I'm doing it. And so can you. Look at a minor league pitcher like Tommy Lasorda, who had a cup of coffee, as a major league pitcher, but enjoyed a feast of National league and World Series Baseball championship titles, as one of Baseball's greatest managers of all time. Nothing is impossible. Ask Tommy Lasorda. He'll tell you otherwise.

Use Technical analysis to help you score at Stock Market Baseball

At the beginning of this book I wrote that I grew my portfolio in 2009 by 500%. My account balance in January of 2009 was a little over $104,000.00. By December of 2009 it was over $555,000.00. 2010 wasn't too bad either. That's why I wrote this book.

Technical analysis didn't make those investments good. There were other aspects of the various stocks that I traded that made them either good, or bad investments. But technical analysis gave me the tools to find them, and to have a better understanding of when to buy them, and when to sell them.

In the game of Stock Market Baseball technical analysis is like knowing how to read your stat sheet to better understand the strengths and weaknesses of the players that are playing for, and against you. And with that information you can decide when to bunt, when to hit to advance your runners, to score, and when to swing for the bleachers.

Dream. Dream Big.

©2013 John George Campbell stockmarketbaseball.com

Dream. Dream Big

When I was a kid playing little league, I never dreamed of playing major league baseball. Never entered my mind. But some kids dreamed that dream, and achieved it. I dreamed about becoming a professional singer, traveling the world, and appearing on TV someday. And I achieved those dreams.

One of my earliest dreams of performing in front of thousands of people was when I was in my teens. I dreamed about performing as a soloist in Los Angeles' Hollywood Bowl. I had never been to the Hollywood Bowl when I dreamed my dream, but I vividly saw myself performing in front of thousands of people in the audience, with the spotlight on me, and a large band behind me, performing at the Hollywood Bowl. I didn't understand the dream at the time, but it did drive my imagination, and set a goal that I wanted to achieve. During my sophomore year in college I entered a regional Battle of the Bands competition that took several months of head to head competition with other singers, in order to win the right to perform in the Hollywood Bowl. I had grown up in a strict Christian upbringing, so much so that I had never performed anything other than sacred, spiritual, and gospel songs in church, or church school, settings. But all of a sudden, I was excelling at performing in settings that didn't care about my church affiliation. The judges were judging on talent, and performance abilities. And I was winning. My eventual performance in the finals of this months long competition was the fulfillment of a dream come true. I had dreamed of this occasion, performing in front of thousands in the audience, years before it happened. And it happened. Just as I had envisioned it.

I bring this up to suggest to you that as the song "Somewhere over the Rainbow [xxxiii]" suggests, "dreams that you care to dream really do come true", IF you care to dream them. If you don't set goals, or have dreams of what you want to achieve in your life, day by day, month by month, and year by year, then you're limiting the possibilities of what you could be, or achieve, in your life.

If learning how to use technical chart analysis, and technical indicators, to trade stocks with, as well as trading for 1%, 2%, 3%, and an occasional home run in stock market baseball can help you to achieve some of your dreams, then I'll be happy with my dream for this book.

About the Author

John George Campbell is a man of many interests, analyzing stock charts being just one of them. By learning to understand the visual information that stock charts and technical indicators were giving him, John increased his portfolio by over 500%, in less than a years time. Other interests include singing, performing on stage, traveling, sports, cooking, art collecting, and especially his business associates, his dogs and cats.

Endnotes and LINKS

---

[i] thinkorswim®, a TDAmeritrade, Inc. related company
https://www.thinkorswim.com/tos/client/index.jsp

[ii] Charles Schwab & Company, Inc. https://www.schwab.com/

[iii] ETrade Financial Corporation
https://us.etrade.com/home

[iv] Saturday Night Live, NBC National Broadcast Company
http://www.nbc.com/saturday-night-live/

[v] ProphetCharts® **Prophet Charts** - Learning Center - Thinkorswim

[vi] ProphetCharts®
[vii] ProphetCharts®

[viii] MSNBC.com. Comprehensive Financial information
http://www.msnbc.com/

[ix] MarketWatch.com. Comprehensive Financial information
http://www.marketwatch.com/

[x] Yahoo.com http://www.yahoo.com/

[xi] Yahoo Finance. Financial information and financial message boards. http://finance.yahoo.com/

[xii] StockTA.com. Simple, easy to understand Technical Analysis site. http://www.stockta.com/cgi-bin/analysis.pl

[xiii] StockConsultant.com
http://www.stockconsultant.com/

[xiv] StockCharts.com
http://stockcharts.com/

[xv] thinkorswim® ProphetCharts®. Great comprehensive technical analysis and charting tools, as well as trading platform. I use this.

[xvi] StockTA.com . Simple Technical Analysis site
http://www.stockta.com/cgi-bin/analysis.pl

[xvii] StockConsultant.com
http://www.stockconsultant.com/

[xviii] FinViz . Comprehensive Stock Screening site. http://finviz.com/

[xix] AmericanBulls.com for Candlestick Chart patterns.
http://www.americanbulls.com/Default.aspx?lang=en

[xx] StockConsultants.com also does a real nice job with it's candlestick charting lessons. Same thing with their P&F, Point and Figure, chart lessons. http://www.stockconsultant.com/

[xxi] Pivot Point Calculator http://www.mypivots.com/investment-calculators/pivot-point-calculator

[xxii] Virtual trading Game at MarketWatch.com
http://www.marketwatch.com/game/

[xxiii] FOREX . Currency and commodities.
http://www.forex.com/

[xxiv] How Charts Can Help You in the Stock Market by William Jiler, OTC publications ©1962. Great , easy to understand book about stock charts.

[xxv] *The Intelligent Investor*, by Benjamin graham. ©1949 Harper Brothers. Classic book on investing.

[xxvi] *Contrarian Investment Strategy* by David Dremen , Free press, 2012

[xxvii] SEEKING ALPHA. Stock Market News and Analysis site..
http://seekingalpha.com/

[xxviii] THE HARD RIGHT EDGE, featuring the insights of Alan Farley. Good site to learn about technical analysis and swing trading. Very informative.
http://www.hardrightedge.com/

[xxix] Securities and Exchange Commission.
http://www.sec.gov/

[xxx] Bloomberg TV http://www.bloomberg.com/tv/shows/

[xxxi] CNBC
http://www.cnbc.com/

[xxxii] FOX Business News http://www.foxbusiness.com/index.html

[xxxiii] Somewhere Over the Rainbow
(From Wikipedia)
Over the Rainbow" (often referred to as **"Somewhere Over the Rainbow"**) is a classic Academy Award-winning ballad, with music by Harold Arlen and lyrics by E.Y. Harburg.[1] It was written for the 1939 movie *The Wizard of Oz*, and was sung by actress Judy Garland in her starring role as Dorothy Gale.[1] Over time, it would become Garland's signature song and, indeed, her theme.

[xxxiv] Headshot of John George Campbell by Patti Robinson Basurto http://pblifephotography.com/

www.ingramcontent.com/pod-product-compliance
Lightning Source LLC
Chambersburg PA
CBHW051809170526
45167CB00005B/1947